Night Fishing For Monster Striped Bass

Night Fishing For Monster Striped Bass

Stories Of The Secretive World Of Bridge Fishing From The West End Bridges Of Long Island's South Shore

Richard Troxler

Disclaimer

The events in this book are meant as entertainment, not as an instructional or how-to guide. Individuals who choose to pursue activities described herein do so at their own risk, and with the express understanding that neither the author, the publisher, or anybody associated with this publication, shall have any liability to any person, or entity, with respect to any loss or damage caused, or alleged to be caused directly or indirectly, by the information contained in this book.

To my wife Cindy, she never said I couldn't go

Table of Contents

Prologue ix

Preface xiii

And So It Begins… 1

Who Is This Guy? 13

The View From The Top… 25

Bridging The Gap… 49

The Great Recovery… 93

Different Strokes & Orbits 101

Big Fish… 139

Post 09/11/01… 173

Goodbye To The 3rd Wantagh Bridge… 207

Epilogue… 225

Acknowledgements 229

About The Author 231

Prologue

All locations mentioned in this book will be specific to Long Island, New York. Some of these locations may have very descriptive information associated with them. Readers of this book who are from Long Island may be familiar with some of these areas, but will probably not be familiar with many of the details described. Obviously, readers not from Long Island will not be familiar with these locations at all. Whichever the case may be, as the author, I have endeavored to make locational descriptions as accurate, and richly detailed as possible, so that your mind's eye can bring you into the scene.

But if you really want to be brought into the scene, and have an actual look at basically all of the locations described in this book, then I have a great suggestion for you. While reading this book, if at all possible, you should have a computer on, and Bing Maps running on your Internet browser. If you don't already have it, just Google "Bing Maps" and it'll be your first result. When you first get on Bing Maps, it'll have some default map loaded, and on the left side of the screen there will be a big pop-out with a bunch of travel related information you don't need. Just click on the left pointing arrow on the right border of the pop-out, about midway down the border, and the pop-out will disappear.

Now you're ready to scroll out until you can get the map small enough to find Long Island, New York, USA. At that point, you put your cursor over Long Island, and start scrolling in over the southern bay areas until you can start reading roads, cities, etc. Wantagh Parkway and Jones Beach are a good place to start. Here's where it gets really interesting! There are three modes that Bing Maps offer, two of which are extremely useful. Early in the book, I'm going to describe the nine bridges that make up what are referred to as the "west end bridges". I describe what their names are and where they are located, and in Bing Maps "Satellite" mode, which recently replaced their "Bird's Eye" mode, you will be able to examine these bridges in great detail. But it gets even better.

In its latest version, Bing Maps now offers a "3D" mode. 3D mode utilizes the high resolution images from the retired Birds Eye mode, along with images from the former "Streetside" mode, adds a little AI, and bingo, amazing 3D views of just about everywhere we fished, from just about any angle. The Satellite and 3D modes are pop out options from the top button located at the upper right of the map. You can zoom in or out using a scroll wheel, or the plus and minus buttons. Just below the plus and minus buttons is the directional arrow that lets you change your view point three hundred and sixty degrees. Between Satellite and 3D modes, you get to see the same roads we traveled, check out many of the views of the bridges we fished from, although several of them have changed radically, or been completely rebuilt since the days we fished them. It'll put you right in the scene. The only thing you'll miss is the mystical, and sometimes scary experience of fishing these bridges in the dead of night.

Now, Bing Maps is not a necessity, as the book can, and does stand on its own, but due to the fact that much of the content of this book is location centric, the technology Bing Maps brings to the table, provides an effective virtual assist to the stories told in this book. So, have some fun with it, and let your imagination take you back, as the days of fishing the west end bridges are gone forever.

Preface

*Two Friends And The Decades They Spent Fishing
The West End Bridges Of Long Island's South Shore*

So, what is this book about? Well, basically this book is about two fishermen who became longtime friends and the stories they have to tell from back in the day, about a unique form of striped bass fishing. Why stories you might ask? The answer to that question is two-fold. First, there is already a wealth of fishing how-to information available at the click of a mouse, as well as at seminars given at the off-season fishing shows. I have a YouTube channel that is well known for my videos on reading the beach and identifying beach structure, but it also has many videos that cover just about every aspect of surf fishing in great detail. You can check it out here if you like: https://www.youtube.com/@richtroxler

Billy has done seminars for decades at just about every major surf fishing show and has one book out about him already *Night Tides – The Fishing Legend of Billy the Greek*. You can find a lot of his lectures and seminars on

YouTube also. There are also many other prominent names in the surf fishing community that have websites, YouTube channels, how-to books, and courses for sale, so there is no shortage of available knowledge out there when it comes to fishing for striped bass. So no, what the world doesn't need is another how-to book on fishing for striped bass from us. That being said, some of the stories you will hear in this book, or some of the conversations that are transcribed in this book, may include techniques, that you, the reader, have never heard about before. In ancient times, knowledge used to be passed on to the next generation through stories, and while we're no longer in ancient times, you may glean some knowledge from our tales of days gone by.

The second reason is this. Something quite mysterious and unexpected has recently happened to both Billy and I. We woke up one morning and realized we aren't in our prime anymore. That's a nice way of saying we got old. Plain and simple, we just can't fish as hard as we used to. We still fish pretty hard, but our bodies just can't take the grind that we used to put them through without blinking an eye. We have to pace ourselves, Lord forbid. We need to recover after a couple late nights. I even sold my Korkers on eBay because the Meniere's Disease in my right ear has ruined my balance, and I don't want to become the very person I used to despise on the jetty, you know, the one who has no business being on the rocks. I mean, C'mon! Getting old sucks!

So, without even fair warning, Billy and I have joined the next generation of old guy fishermen, so what good are we now? Well, what Billy and I have discovered is one thing that the generations of fishermen behind us want from us is stories from back in the day. And the one topic they REALLY want to know about is fishing from atop and around the west end bridges, something we NEVER talked about back then. During the peak of the striped bass recovery, most serious striped bass fishermen had heard the rumors of the fantastic fishing around the bridges. Whether it was small talk in the local bait and tackle stores, or phone calls from friends, word got around. It was hard to keep that kind of fishing a secret. In fact, the fishing was so good that those rumors managed to propagate forward through time, to a whole new generation of striped bass fishermen.

But in our opinion, the reason the bridges never got crowded back then, was that for the average fisherman, walking out onto an unknown bridge for the first time, in the middle of the night, all by yourself, without a clue as to what to do, or how to do it, was simply too intimidating for the average person. Most fishermen at that time, would claim it wasn't their thing, or they only fished in the surf, or were plug fishing purists. It didn't matter that we were pulling huge numbers of big fish, night after night, and that the bay was overflowing with bass. They all knew the fish were there, they'd drive by slowly in their trucks, in the middle of the night, and take a look, but most just kept on going, and having gone through the learning process myself, I can't say I blame them.

So, when Billy and I get in one-on-one conversations with other fishermen from that time and general area, inevitably the questions turn to the bridges. They want to know how the hell did you catch bass from atop the bridges, how many fish a night did you catch, was it really as good as the rumors, did people get hit by cars, did the police arrest you guys, tow your vehicles, did anybody ever fall from them, and they want to know EVERYTHING about what the glory days of the 90s and early 2K were like on the bridges!

And they should know. Why? Because simply put, they are never going to have nights like that again, EVER! Sadly, for reasons we will touch on, it is the fate of the striped bass biomass that it will never recover to those historic numbers again. The post moratorium, perfect storm, of large, successful year classes, from both the Chesapeake and Hudson stocks, produced a biomass of striped bass so massive, that by the late 90s and into 2000, they were almost everywhere, all at once. They lined the inlets, filled the bays, rivers, LI Sound, Montauk, North Fork, up the coast, down the coast, everybody had fish. If you couldn't catch a striped bass back then, you probably weren't trying very hard. But those days of plenty have passed, gone the way of the Dodo.

With the collapse of the striped bass biomass, coupled with the political changes that came after September 11, 2001, the mystical age of fishing from atop the West End bridges is another era whose days have come and gone, never to be repeated. That fishing was so insane, so incredibly good, yet so difficult to master, that it'll be hard to describe it to the uninitiated, but Billy and I will tell you about those incredible nights and what made those bridges so magical, and so evil. The stories in this book are not just about catching fish, instead, they try to encapsulate the entire bridge fishing experience based on our many decades of fishing them. Between Billy and I, we have enough stories to fill three books the size of *War and Peace,* so deciding what stories to include in order to accomplish that goal was not an easy process.

The format of this book is that it doesn't really have a format. It might be roughly chronological at times, but don't count on it, particularly with the humorous little stories that are added, just because they are funny. As the actual author, a lot of it may be written in the past or present tense from my perspective, some may be past or present tense in Billy's perspective, and a lot of it is just going to be direct transcriptions from actual recorded phone conversations that Billy and I have had:

Billy: You know, one night in 2008 I caught five Bass over fifty pounds and one of them was over sixty!

Rich: Yeah right!

Fact check — Billy actually did, it was June 5, 2008!

One more thing. Billy and I both use very colorful language, but colorful language doesn't read well, so it's been left out except where really necessary, and even then, it's abbreviated, or imitated. I'm shooting for G-rated here. So sit back and enjoy this trip back in time.

This was the last time I fished with Billy before moving to Virginia. It was 2014 and I had found some fish out at Cupsogue Beach.

And So It Begins…

The reflection of white clouds and blue sky on the surface of the mirror smooth water was suddenly shattered, as a giant bluefish smashed the beat-up old popper I was getting ready to lift into the boat. The suddenness of the strike in the early morning calmness made me jump involuntarily, and a wry smile creased my lips as I glanced over at Billy to see if he had noticed. As chance would have it, he had noticed, and he wasted no time busting my chops at how I had missed the hit and had managed to get my plug tangled up in the boat's anchor rope behind me in the bow.

At that point in time, I hadn't known Billy for very long, and as that was my first time fishing with him, I had wanted to make a good impression, you know, male egos and all. But in retrospect, what really stands out in my mind, once again due to chance, is the completely impromptu conditions that had made that trip possible, because if not for the strange convergence of events that resulted in that trip, I may never have become friends with Billy, and an entire, incredibly important part of my fishing and personal life, would have never come to past.

People, in general, like to think that they are the captains of their ship, masters of their own destiny, large and in charge of their world and all that's in it. But that's not reality, at least not in the mathematical sense. When we look back in time, most of us never realize how large a part random chance has played in the shaping of our lives. Think about it for a second. Friends, spouses, children, sometimes jobs, fortunes, even life or death, can all fall within the realm of chance, a simple spin of the wheel. Basically, we all pinball through our lives, making the best of what chance has to offer, while steering our ships as best we can.

So it was through random chance that I came to meet Billy Legakis aka Billy the Greek for the first time, during a 9-ball tournament at the now defunct Mr. Cue Billiards in Lindenhurst, New York. This was actually two convergent elements of chance. The first was that Billy and I, aside from being avid fishermen, are both avid pool players, and the second element of chance was that I would wind up with him as my opponent in the 2nd round of the tournament. What are the chances LOL.

But that magic moment, that nexus that would bind these elements of chance together and begin our friendship, had yet to reveal itself. For I had no knowledge of Billy other than as some guy I had seen occasionally around the pool rooms, and I was certainly not aware of his reputation as a well-known striped bass fisherman. Likewise, Billy knew me only as the night house man of Bayshore Billiards, and had no way of knowing of my passion for fishing, as we fished different areas of Long Island. At that point, Billy was just some guy, it was just a 9-ball match, race to five, and I was losing.

Then the magic word came out, the wheel of chance stopped, and the bell went off. Billy, who had won the last game, broke on the next game, but failed to drop any balls on the break, so it was my turn at the table. As he walked to his chair he remarked disgustedly, "I don't know why I'm even playing tonight, I should be fishing." DING went the bell. I stopped in mid stride.

"Fishing?" I asked. "What are you fishing for?"

Billy just kind of waved off the question but said, "There's bass all over the bridges, it's stupid fishing."

With my break the last thing on my mind, I asked what bridges he was talking about, but he told me that he wasn't really supposed to talk about it. That was not the answer I wanted to hear, and Billy wasn't going to get off that easy. Over the next several games I observed proper billiards etiquette and remained silent while he was at the table. But as soon as it became my turn, I started in on him again about the bridges, and eventually persuaded him to tell me more about them during the rest of the match, which of course, I subsequently lost. Losing the match didn't matter because I was hooked, pun intended. Catching bass from atop those bridges was all I could think about now.

So that is how Billy and I became acquainted. I would put the date around 1987, not long after the movie *The Color Of Money* (1986) had come out. The reason this sticks out in my mind is because that movie had caused a remarkable upsurge in the popularity of pool. Pool halls went from relatively quiet, to long wait times for tables every night, in a relatively short period of time, so it's about the best time stamp I can come up with. I personally have almost no relationship with time, I never have, which by default means it is very difficult for me to associate dates to the sequence of events in my life's chronology. Sometimes I'm not even sure of the order some events have happened in. Needless to say, this is a source of endless frustration to my wife, of I'm not sure how many years, because I can't remember the year we got married.

What I do remember about that time was that the company I worked for had gone under several months earlier and I was taking an early mid-life vacation before joining the work force again. In other words, I was in total free spool. I was friends with the owner of Bayshore Billiards, the late Keith (KC) Jones, a great man and may he rest in peace, and when I became unemployed, KC offered me the position of night house man at Bayshore Billiards, which I gratefully accepted. As perks, I played for free, anytime, day or night, and after I closed at 2:00 a.m. I could run money games all night until the cows came home. And with the popularity of the movie *The Color Of Money* causing every rank amateur in town to fall into the Tom Cruise syndrome, the pickings were easy and plentiful.

So that was my life at that point in time. Unmarried, with a roughly ten-year relationship recently ended, I was playing the field, living off the pool cue, fishing, pretty much unencumbered by anything, other than the nights I

4

had to work at the pool hall. Yup, total free spool. Working late nights, and frequently playing after hour money games until sun up, might be a difficult adjustment for many people, but for me it came easy. I was already preconditioned. From the time I left home at seventeen to seek my fame and fortune in rock and roll, right up to that very point in time, where I had spent many late nights fishing, and still playing musical gigs off and on, I had always been a night person. My roaring metabolism never needed more than 4 hours sleep a night, and a quick nap at some point to get by. Of course, on weekends I didn't get out of bed until 5:00 p.m. in the afternoon. So, working the night shift was no big deal for me.

However, working nights did cause an interesting paradigm shift in my fishing schedule. Prior to that period in my life, the only sunrise fishing I had ever done was if I had stayed out on a tide all night long. And that was a fairly rare experience. But I found that with working nights, when the money games ended early, or there were none, which sometimes happened, I would head out fishing and frequently catch the sunrise and morning bite. It was an interesting learning experience for me, as well as treating me to some amazing eye candy, in the form of many beautiful sunrises.

Several weeks after my fateful meeting with Billy, I was down at Mr. Cue Billiards in Lindenhurst on one of my nights off. It was fairly late, and I was playing solo on the house table, which is located near the front entrance and main window. I looked out the window and saw Billy coming toward the door with another one of the regulars, a young Spanish guy, nice kid. The kid looked excited, gesturing with his hands, very animated, and as Billy opened the door, I could hear by the kid's voice that he was indeed, very excited about something. So, I stopped shooting and as they came in, I said, "Hey" to them both and asked what was going on. The kid proceeded to go straight into telling me about how Billy took him up on one of the bridges, so that he could catch a bass for his mother for dinner. He went on to say that he caught a couple bass, how awesome it was, blah, blah, blah, but at that point I was no longer listening.

Although I have never admitted this to Billy until committing this to print, I definitely felt a twinge of envy toward the kid that night. Although I had expressed interest in finding out what fishing from the bridges was all about, I had not pressed the issue very hard, basically for fear of being told to go piss off. Since Billy had told me about it, it had been burning a hole in my brain. I had become quite obsessed with the whole concept of bridge fishing, and visions of giant bass languishing in the shadow lines cast by the lights on the bridges, had visited my day dreams daily. But I also realized that I really didn't know Billy very well, and even if I flat out asked him, he certainly had no obligation to show me anything he didn't want to. So that night, with the bass season nearly ended, I figured that the window of opportunity had closed on making my day dreams a reality for that year. Perhaps next year, I thought, if chance were to smile upon me, maybe then I might be able to get him to show me the ropes.

The striped bass season closed and winter passed uneventfully into spring, and then into early summer. I occasionally saw Billy around the pool rooms during that time, but I don't remember us having a whole lot of in-depth conversations, mostly just pool or fishing small talk. It was at some point in the summer that KC, the owner of Bayshore Billiards, decided to re-do the interior of the pool hall. As part of that process, the walls would be re-painted, and as Billy was a professional painter, and KC's friend, he was the man for the job.

The catch was that the painting would take place at night, after the pool hall closed at 2:00 a.m. At that point I began seeing Billy every night. He would paint while the various money games went on, and if the games ended early, or there were no games, I would hang around a while and shoot the bs with him. It was one such night that the wheel of chance stopped again and everything fell into alignment.

That night, myself, and three other regulars, played a couple games of Chicago before calling it quits at around 3:00 a.m. or so. Everybody left, so I cleaned the table and was just getting ready to sit down when Billy looked down from the ladder and said, "I don't feel like painting tonight, you want to go fishing?"

"Fishing?" I wasn't even sure I had heard him right.

"Yeah, fishing," Billy replied. "I got something I think you'd really like. Can you drive a boat?"

"Yeah, I can drive a boat. Why?"

7

"Just in case I want to sleep on the way back."

"Sleep on the way back? Where the hell are we going?"

"You'll see," he said.

I was totally pumped. The first stop was the diner down a block from the pool hall for breakfast. Over breakfast, Billy told me we'd make a stop at my place and I should grab a medium spinning rod for casting from a boat. He said not to worry about tackle, that he had that covered. We finished breakfast quickly, and headed to my place. I grabbed my bunker snagging outfit, which had a small bucktail tied on, which I had been using for shore bound fluke fishing. I also brought a medium conventional casting outfit just for good measure, and then we were off to where the boat was docked.

It was just starting to get light when we arrived at the boat. I loaded my rods on, we threw the lines, and headed out in the small center console. I had no idea as to where we were going, but when we made it out to the main channel, Billy opened it up, and we were on our way. I also didn't know what we were going to be fishing for, but I knew all would be revealed in time. I don't remember how long we ran for, but we eventually stopped by a railroad bridge. Billy proceeded to pull the boat right up to a piling, saw the bucktail on my rod and said, "May I?"

"Sure, go for it."

He lobbed a cast back past the piling as we drifted slowly away with the tide. He let the bucktail drop for a few seconds and then flipped the bail on the reel. The bucktail never even made it to the bottom before it got hit. Billy set the hook, the rod bent, and then the fight was over before it ever got going. Billy reeled in the line and confirmed that the bucktail had been bitten off.

"Bluefish," he said. "Felt like a big one." Looking at the line again, he asked, "Where's your leader?"

"I don't have one," I said.

"You don't have a leader?"

"No, I don't have a leader. I use that rod for snagging bunker mostly, what do I need a leader for?" It might have sounded a tad defensive, you know, male egos and all, but it wasn't really meant to be.

"But you had a bucktail tied on, you snag bunker with a bucktail?" At that point I knew he was just breaking my balls, so I just nodded, touché. Getting to know people is a nerve-wracking process sometimes.

"I was fluking," I said. "There's a couple nice sandbars in the State Channel around Oak Island. They've been stacked there like cord wood."

Smiling, Billy said, "Fluke have teeth you know."

"Yeah, I know they have teeth, but that's 20 lb. test on there and I've never had a Fluke bite me off yet, so if it's OK with you, I think I'm good." A little jab back for good measure.

With that, Billy leaned down and pulled out a spool of leader material from his bag.

"Well, you're going to need a leader where we're going." He clipped off a length of leader material and deftly joined one end to my running line. To the other end he tied on a big, old, beat-up popper, obviously intended to be that day's sacrificial lamb. Considering it was summer, I think I had a pretty good idea of what the target species of the day was going to be.

9

As soon as Billy finished rigging up the rods, he fired up the outboard again and we took off west, down what I now know was Reynolds Channel. After a short distance, we turned right and headed into back bay waters. At that point, the sun had just cleared the horizon and it was dead calm, not a breath of wind anywhere. We idled along slowly for quite a long time, heading deeper into the bay. I clearly saw through the placid surface of the water, that it was no more than a couple feet deep, or so it seemed, as super clear water can sometimes play tricks on your vision, especially when you had been up all night.

Slowly idling along and staring at the bottom, had eventually become hypnotic, so when Billy killed the engine, I kind of snapped out of my reverie. He told me to throw the anchor, which was in the bow, and tie it off. Throwing the anchor further confirmed the fact, that we were in very shallow water. After I tied off the anchor, I remember kind of just standing there for a couple of seconds thinking to myself, *So here we are, deep in a bay, in the middle of nowhere, anchored on acres of two-foot shallow flats, now what?*

Billy, on the other hand, wasted no time in picking up his rod, which I remember had an old Crack spinning reel on it, and lobbing a popper far off into the bay. It splashed down in the calm water causing rings of water to emanate away from it, before he started his rhythmic retrieve to the boat. I figured that was the plan for the day, so I grabbed my rod and followed suit. Nothing happened for either of us on our first couple casts, but then as I was just getting ready to cast my plug Billy called out.

"Rich, check it out! He's stalking my plug!"

It took me a second to locate his plug, which was still a fairly long way from the boat, but I could clearly see the bluefish's fins and wake following Billy's plug.

"He's just following it, but he hasn't made up his mind yet. Look! You see his tail!" Billy said excitedly.

"Yeah, I see it", I said. "How can you miss it?"

Billy made some fast twitches to the popper and sped up his retrieve with some more commotion, and that made up the fish's mind. The big bluefish closed the distance in an instant, crashed the water's surface with an explosive strike, and the fight was on. Now I could give you an adjective filled version of the battle that followed, but the truth is, I don't remember the exact details of the battle other than Billy, after a prolonged fight, finally grabbing the leader and flipping a giant bluefish into the boat, so I'll just move on instead. Billy and I fished for about an hour or so, and we each had several big bluefish before the gnats reminded us of our place in the food chain, and drove us out.

Now, these weren't just *big* bluefish, these were *gator* bluefish, upper teen size, solo fish. What those fish were doing back there at that time of year I have no idea, and to the best of my knowledge, neither does Billy, but he's known about them since he was a kid. I wrote an article years ago called "In Praise of Bluefish" where I pointed out that bluefish frequently get treated like a second-class sport fish. That morning with Billy reminds me of how undeserved that reputation truly is. Bluefish that size are

11

mean, extremely powerful fish, that never quit, and experiencing them burning off many yards of line in a matter of seconds, in shallow water, leaving wakes as they went, and tearing up the surface attacking those plugs, was in my mind, nothing less than a world-class fishing experience. As Billy told me while we were wrapping it up and getting ready to leave, "It's the closest thing you can get to Florida flats fishing on Long Island."

I pulled the anchor and we made our way off the flats and headed west down Reynolds Channel to the Atlantic Beach Bridge, which is right before you head out of East Rockaway Inlet. We threw bucktails for a short period of time before calling it a morning. We headed back the way we came and eventually Billy pulled the boat up to a dock and tied it off. I followed him off the dock and up some stairs where we entered a large building, a bait station of sorts was my guess. He said, "Hi" to a women who was cleaning a table, and as he strode toward the back luncheon counter, he turned to me and asked if I was hungry.

I thought he was offering to buy me something. But as I was telling him that I was fine, he had already made his way behind the counter and was headed toward a large refrigerator that was against the back wall. He opened the refrigerator and took out two eggs and butter, walked down to the grill, smeared some butter on the grill, and started frying the eggs! Then he pulls a roll out of a large plastic bag and cuts it in half for the eggs. As he's flipping his eggs, I remember standing there, my tired brain trying to process everything I was seeing, and thinking to myself, *Who is this guy?* Well, as I would learn much later on, the answer to that question began with the very building I was standing in.

When Billy would catch a fifty he would often run across the street to the beach and pose for the picture in waders with a spinning rod, so that people would think he caught it on the beach.

These are the rocks that run down the side of the southwest side of the 2nd Wantagh Bridge. They are nowhere near as sketchy as the rocks that went down the sides of the old 3rd Wantagh Bridge. This picture was adapted from a color 3D screen shot from Bing Maps and appears to have been taken while the 2nd underwent reconstruction. Note the lack of a railing.

Who Is This Guy?

That building, the one I had been standing in all those years ago, in my state of confusion and wonderment, was Frank's Fishing Station. The "Frank" in Frank's Fishing Station was Frank Dominic, who opened up his operation on Harbor Isle, in Island Park, Long Island in 1938. Among other things, Franks Fishing Station was the wholesale supplier of bait to all the bait & tackle shops, as well as the charter / party boat fleets, in the entire area. Billy's first job was working for the Commodore Fishing Fleet, just opposite Frank's Fishing Station. At that time, the Commodore Fishing fleet was a large enterprise consisting of three party boats, one hundred or so rental skiffs, dockage, and bait and tackle. Billy had worked there since he was a kid, as a mate on the party boats, setting up skiffs, receiving bait, and performing various other tasks.

The fascinating thing about random chance is that we never really identify it, give it a second thought, or a moment's consideration. But it's always there, and in many instances, it makes the most important decisions in our lives for us, without us even being aware of it. Sometimes it revolves around the simplest of things imaginable. Take bait for example. What could be more inconsequential in our lives, than bait? But for Billy, back in the days of the Commodore Fleet, bait was a nexus, a cross-point. Frank delivered it, Billy received it, and it was through that nexus that Billy entered Frank's world, and where his real education as a striped bass fisherman began. Here's how Billy tells it:

Billy: I was working at the Commodore Fishing Station at the base of the Long Beach bridge, and Frank at the time, was the sole bait distributor in the area for all the party boats. He supplied ground bunker, clam chum, caught Spearing, Killies, everything, and that's what he did, he was a commercial bait guy, and a premier striped bass fisherman. He was like the legend of his day, everybody knew him, he was the best of the striped bass fishermen that we knew of. So, ah, Frank used to deliver bait to the Commodore Fishing Station, and I'd take the bait, pack it all away, you know. Frank always liked me because I was a good worker, I minded my business and worked hard. So, I guess I was around fourteen at the time, Frank says, "Hey kid, why don't you come to work for me." I mean, I really liked John at the Commodore, and even then, I was always loyal and never sold anybody out, and John knew I wanted to be a bass fisherman, because a bunch of the guys from the Commodore used

16

to take me bass fishing, you know what I mean, since I was a little kid, they'd take me clam chumming.

So, I went and I told John, "Frank, Frank wants me to work." I was so excited, "Frank wants me to work for him," you know, and that's not exactly the right thing to say to your boss. [*laughing*] But John was a real cool guy, and he knew I wanted to catch bass, so he says, "Listen, Frank is like the best bass fisherman in the world, go ahead and go to work for him if he wants you to." And I did.

I learned more at Frank's, in fact, it was because of Frank that I became the bass fisherman that I am today, literally, because of our ability to catch bait! Frank, he was there since 1938, he knew every piece of bait in the bay, he knew when it came in, when it left, he knew all of that, so as I started to work with him catching bait, I started to learn all that, and then I understood why the fish were where they were, you just kind of got a different outlook on it, you know.

And then Frank started taking me bass fishing, and he was a bait fisherman. We fished Long Beach, Atlantic Beach, and the Rockaways, especially the Rockaways. The Rockaways were big in those days. You know, the best part about the Rockaways was that you had all those jetties, all the way down to Breezy, you know. And in the boat, in the ocean, hardly anybody fished it in those days. First of all, there weren't many bass fisherman, hardly anybody fished over there, so you'd go out there, and if

17

you saw two or three boats a day, it was a lot. There was nobody out there, and man were there bass out there!

Frank was the one who taught me how to fish live bunker on the jetties, we would catch the bunker and cast them into the jetties from the boat. He taught me how to chunk, all that stuff, how to clam chum. We were so good at clam chumming it was scary. And I really mean that. There were days where we did well over one hundred and fifty fish a day, I mean way over. You know, to catch a hundred fish on a tide was nothing when the fish were there. We didn't talk numbers because most people would tell you you're full of sh!t. All we did was sell fish, there was no other reason to catch'em.

You know, it was a different world in those days, the Long Island Fisherman wasn't even in existence yet, you know what I mean, there were no magazines telling me how to, when to, where to, even when the Fisherman first came out, it was just a BS little magazine. Nobody had any real information chain, so if you kept your mouth shut, you could beat those fish up, I mean really beat'em up.

I remember one time with Jeff and I, we were at Skippy's. When I ran Frank's, Skippy ran Henning's, which was a big fishing station under the Atlantic Beach bridge. Skippy left Henning's and opened up his own tackle shop in East Rockaway. Jeff and I were in there one day, and there were a bunch of other guys there also. Frank and I used to commercially fish the Atlantic Beach bridge, clam chumming, and in those days Frank was the sole supplier of clam chum, he literally brought clam bellies to Long Island, so, we got really good at clam chumming. But anyway, this is years later, so we're in Skippy's and there's some guys there, and they're all talking about clam chumming the Atlantic Beach bridge. I'd done that every day for years when the bass were there, so they're all talking and this one guy says, "Yeah, I've been fishing that bridge for years and I've never had more than twenty-five fish on a tide." So, everyone's talking back and forth and one of the guys knew I fished it commercially years ago, so he goes, "Bill, you used to fish that bridge, how'd you do on it?" I said, "We did great on it." I didn't really want to get into the numbers because once you do that you get into a lot of bullsh!t. So, it goes back and forth a little bit and that one guy goes, "C'mon Bill, what did you really do?" I said, "Okay, when the fish are there, I'll do a hundred fish with my eye's closed." So that guy goes, "You're full of sh!t." [laughs]

So, we go back and forth a little bit and I say, "Okay, we'll go out on your boat." Me, Jeff, Him, and another guy I knew, went out on his boat. The very first day I had around ninety fish, he had three, the next day I went over one hundred twenty-five and stopped counting, by the third day I had this guy talking to himself, I was like, it's all because you don't know how to do this. We clam chummed differently back then, one day I'll tell you about that, it was a whole different ball game than they do it today. Even the way they teach it. Like my version of life is I've never met anyone in my life that clam chums the

19

way we did. Never. There's a lot of things you just don't want to give away, even now [laughs].

We did it (clam chumming) at that time, you got to remember, they didn't want big fish, the market wanted those little fish. When I first started bass fishing, striped bass was fifteen cents a pound for large and twenty-five cents a pound for small fish, so we wanted small fish. And that bridge had a ton of those little eight, nine-pound fish, there were a ton of them there. Like I said, Frank brought clam chumming to Long Island. He got the clam chum from Doxsee Clam Company, out on the island. They were the discards they didn't use for their food products. They would put it in fifty gallon drums and ship them to Frank and we would put them in five gallon gold tins and freeze them. Anyway, when we would fish, we would have those fish piled up ten feet behind the boat, and if you did it right those fish would stay right there and never move.

Rich: What were you using on your hook, clam bellies?

Billy: No, I'd just grab a couple pieces of stringy slim, wrap it around my hook a couple times, and float it out in the tide. Oh, and in those days, I ground all the barbs off every hook I had, not for the reason of conservation, but for the reason of speed. In other words, when you pulled a fish in the boat, as soon as they hit the deck the hook fell right out of their mouth. You didn't have to waste the time unhooking every fish, you just grabbed some more bait and got right back at it. It was a numbers game.

Rich: So Frank Dominic, I guess he pretty much took you in like family, yes?

Billy: Yeah, well what happened is me and Frank hit it off pretty good. I was a good worker, and his son Frank Jr was a great worker, like the hardest working guy, which is rare for a boss's son. We worked at the station every day so we all got along really well, we were real good friends.

Rich: And he gave you free run of the place?

Billy: I had full run of the place. I had the keys to the freezers, the coolers, I could take all the bait I wanted, I could take whatever boat I wanted, you know, like it was mine. The boat I took you to catch those bluefish that day, that was one of Frank's boats.

Rich: I didn't know that! And of course, you could cook yourself an egg sandwich whenever you wanted. [laughing]

Billy: And I could make myself an egg sandwich whenever I felt like it. [*laughs*] You know one of the reasons Frank liked me is because I became really good at what I did, really quick, you know what I mean. I was one of those really aggressive kids as far as catching fish, like before you stopped the boat, I had a fish on. In those

21

days we always used to bet on first fish, most fish, biggest fish, and I would win all three ninety percent of the time, and first fish one hundred percent of the time. I was always in the water before the boat would stop. But Frank liked that about me.

To be honest with you, the best compliment I ever got, in my opinion, was from Frank. And I've never really said this to anybody, but I'll say it to you, and I don't even know if I want you to print this or not, so I'll just say it to you... So, years later I'm in my mid to late thirties, and at that time I was a premier bass fisherman already, I had this sh!t down pat, I was really good at it, and everyone was there. Ronnie (Lepper) the guy who did the bunker spoons, he owned the Charter boat Kim, did nothing but troll spoons, he was one of the pioneers of trolling bunker spoons, Joe Beada was there, Frank Dominic, it was about 7 or 8 of the older guys there, that were real hard core bass fishermen. And I fished with every one of them, and every one of them fished differently. Frank was strictly bait, Skip was a bucktailer, Ronnie Lepper was a troller, you know, they all fished different ways, and they were all talking like, who's the best bass fisherman of the bunch, you know, they were all older now, like in their sixties and seventies, and they're like C'mon Frank, who's the best. Frank turns to'em and says, "The kids the best of all of us," he goes, "he's fished with every one of us, he learned all our stuff, he knows what all of us know, and more."

To me, that was the best compliment I ever got. But even to this day, if you ever asked me, I would never say a bad word about Frank or even consider if I was better than him. To me, he was the best bass fisherman I ever met. Frank caught so many fifty and sixty pound bass and he never took a picture of his fish. He just sold them. I have the only picture I've ever seen of Frank. The one in my book with that big bass in the beginning, I had just happened to have bought a Polaroid camera and took that picture. That was it, there were no pictures of him.

And we shipped thousands of pounds of bass to market, thousands of pounds, and what I mean by that is not just us personally, we all caught fish, but also the other pin hookers, there weren't many of them, maybe about a half a dozen, and all the gill netters too, they would all drop their fish off and we'd pack'em out and ship'em to the market. And the way it worked was real simple. Say you were a pin hooker and you come into the dock and you got 290 pounds of bass. I'd weigh'em up, 290 pounds, I'd give you a slip, 290 pounds. Frank would sell them, whatever the going price was, and he took a percentage, like five percent. So, he would take his five percent and he would give you the rest in cash, and he was as honest as the day is long, so everybody respected him because he never screwed anybody, and you always got paid. So, they didn't even waste time, they just came in and dumped the fish, I'd weigh'em up, give them a slip, and they'd leave. Then we'd pack'em out and ship'em to market. We'd have thousands of fish a week coming into that place. He had some operation in those days. And he was the only one doing it.

Rich: So who taught you to bucktail?

Billy: Actually, Skip Gerdes was a bucktailer and he ran Henning's under the Atlantic Beach bridge. He was a bucktailer right, but he really didn't teach me…he used it, he caught fish on it, and then I started to fish it and I really got good at it as I started to comprehend it.

Rich: But with Frank it was all bait?

Billy: With Frank we fished bait. Frank taught me how to bait fish. Like when we fished live bait, we hooked everything through the nostril, because Frank showed me how bass take bait and why. He said if you hook it in the back, if it doesn't go all the way down the fish's throat, you can pull it out and not hook'em, but if a bass takes your bait and runs, and you got it hooked in the nostril, you don't miss a single fish.

You know, Frank's solely responsible for why I fish the bridges too. He wasn't a bridge fisherman, he knew nothing about it, but I was on Frank's boat one night when this old man on top of the bridge hooked a big fish, you could hear it splashing around. Then as I was watching, he started walking the fish down. I remember saying to Frank, what the f#$%$ is that guy doing? He had no idea. Frank wasn't a bridge fisherman, in those days no one really knew about bridges, fishing off the top, you know what I mean. So I snuck up there, and I found out. That was early in my life, back in the 60s.

The View From The Top…

After Billy's eggs were done, he flipped them on to the waiting roll, sprinkled on some salt and pepper and closed up his sandwich. He took the butter back to the refrigerator and returned with a couple bottles of water, one of which he tossed across the counter to me. He picked up his sandwich, took a bite, and through a mouthful of egg said, "Let's go." I have to admit that after having smelled those eggs cooking, I regretted not taking Billy up on his offer for a second breakfast. We left the way we came, hopped into the center console, threw the lines, and made the short trip back to where the boat was docked. Upon docking we off-loaded everything, gave the boat a quick spray down, grabbed our gear, and headed for our respective rides. I had a long trip home and I was pretty tired by then, so I didn't engage in much small talk other than to thank Billy for the trip and say that I would see him later on that night. I was lucky I didn't fall asleep on the drive home.

That night I showed up a little before my 10:00 pm shift. As bad as I am with time and all, I am fairly certain that it was a Thursday night. The night went as any other night, except I was anxious for it to end, because there was a very important piece of business that I wanted to get out of the way later that night. Billy showed up a little before the 2:00 am closing time, and we talked about that morning's fishing trip while I brush cleaned the unused tables. 2:00 am came, I clocked out the remaining tables, informed the regulars that there would be no after hour games that night, pushed them all out the door and locked it. Billy had just finished spreading some tarps when I walked up to him and said, "Billy, you got minute?"

"Sure, what's on your mind?"

"You know, ever since you told me about fishing on those bridges, it's all I've been thinking about."

"Yeah, I could tell," he said.

"Well, seeing as I'm going to go up on them anyway, I would really appreciate it if you could kinda give me the nickel tour, you know, show me the ropes so that I'll know what I'm up against. Could you do that?"

The two seconds he took to answer seemed like an hour.

"Yeah, I'll do that, but under one condition," he said. "You have to promise that you'll never tell anybody that it was me that told you about fishing the bridges. There are only a handful of us that do it, and some of these guys are pretty nasty, they don't like new guys coming up on the bridges. They might try and run you off, I don't know, so you're on your own. If you see me up there, you don't know me, at least for the time being, so you need to be OK with that, are we clear?"

Talk about a warm welcome.

I nodded my head. "Yeah, I got it."

"Good," Billy said as he once again continued spreading tarps on the floor. "Are you working this Sunday night?"

"Nah, I'm off."

"Do you know where the Dunkin' Donuts on Merrick Road is, in Wantagh?" he asked.

"No idea."

"OK, it's on Merrick Road about a half mile west of the Wantagh Parkway, on the left side. It comes up fast on a turn, so keep your eyes peeled or you'll blow right past it. Meet me there at 9:00 o'clock. Bring a conventional setup, as long a rod as you have, and some bucktails, like two to three ounces. I don't expect fish to be there, it's too early for that. You got all that?"

"I got it, an 8 foot rod okay?"

"Yeah, that'll do for now."

Billy returned to the business of painting and I got back to the business of cleaning tables and putting pool cues away, after which I sat and listened intently as Billy talked about what fishing the bridges was like. All I can remember is that Sunday could not arrive fast enough. But arrive it did. I remember settling on a fairly long rod that I used for blackfish, my second favorite fish, matched with a Daiwa Mag Force reel loaded with thirty pound Ande mono line. I found the D&D without incident and was there a half hour early. Billy showed up shortly after. On that warm, humid, August night, we piled into my Grand Am, rods sticking out the passenger window, and off we went to pop my bridge fishing cherry.

27

There are nine bridges, all within five minutes of each other, that make up the group of what is generally referred to, as the *west end* bridges. There are three bridges on the Wantagh Parkway that cross out to the eastern end of Jones Beach State Park. Going from north to south, they are referred to as The 1st (Flat or Seaman's Creek Bridge), 2nd (Goose Creek Bridge), and 3rd (Sloop Channel Bridge) Wantagh bridges respectively. Then there are the three bridges on the Meadowbrook Parkway that cross to the western end of Jones Beach State Park. These too, run north to south with the northern most bridge being commonly referred to as The 1st Meadowbrook (Glenn Curtiss Bridge), the middle bridge, The Fundy Bridge, and the southern-most bridge, The Meadowbrook Bridge aka Big M. The last three bridges are on the Loop Parkway, which runs west off of Jones Island, between The Fundy Bridge and The Big M. The first bridge you cross leaving Jones Island is The Swift Creek Bridge, the second bridge you cross is the Loop Parkway Draw Bridge, and the last bridge is the Point Lookout Bridge. It was these bridges that made up my Sunday night tour.

After leaving Dunkin' Donuts we drove east to the Wantagh Parkway and got on heading South. By the time I reached the parkway speed limit, the lights from the baseball fields in Wantagh Park, to my right, were lighting up the night sky, with small clouds of fog from the nearby bay hanging around each grouping. As the last of the lights passed, we crossed a small bridge onto Great Island and Billy told me to pull over and park on the shoulder. This was the 1st Wantagh Bridge. We got out, but left the rods in the car. Billy just wanted to quickly show me this bridge and told me that nobody really fished this bridge from the top.

We walked over to the bridge, which was indeed small, and he starting giving me a brief history of the bridge. But to be honest, I can't recall a word he said. I had never seen any part of the west end bay system at night before, and I wasn't prepared for the effect it was going to have on me. As I looked out at the miles of channels, the islands, the black moving water, the misty darkness, the reflections of distant lights, the sod banks, the intriguing shoreline around the bridge, and the rips off the nearby point, I stood transfixed, taking everything in, all at once, like a drug hit. After the initial rush passed, I remember thinking, *Screw line-ups on the jetty, jockeying for spots on the beach during a sand eel or mullet run, and crowds at the sandbar, THIS will be my playground!*

We then crossed the parkway to take a look at the other side. It was this side, the east side, that had the bike path with the high chain link fence along the outer edge, so that people riding their bikes couldn't accidentally fall off the bridge. Billy explained that this bike path went all the way out to Jones Beach. While looking around the area, I noticed that there was a small little pathway that disappeared into the brush, that likely led to the shore area below. I had noticed one on the other side of the bridge also. They called to me, and I knew that it would not be long before I went down both of them.

We then returned to my car and continued south for about a mile to the 2nd Wantagh Bridge. I was instructed to drive over the bridge and then park on the grassy shoulder area on the southwest side of the bridge. We grabbed our rods and walked along a waist high chain link fence until we reached the base of the bridge. Back then, the 2nd Wantagh was a drawbridge, which had a walkway on its west side, that went out to a square concrete island of sorts. This is where one side of the iron-grate type draw bridge was connected and the walkway ended. The chain link fence we had walked along was connected to a heavy steel pipe railing at the base of the bridge where the walkway began. The railing ran along the water-side edge of the walkway and the concrete island. The top railing was also about waist high and the middle railing was about knee high. The highway side of the walkway consisted of those concrete barrier sections you see everywhere, like dividing lanes at toll booths and re-routing traffic during construction, those things.

We walked out onto the bridge with our rods in hand. Billy lead the way and I followed. I tried to make sure that I didn't spear him with my rod because my eyes were looking at everything except where I was going. I was awestruck. This was fishing from a totally new angle, literally, and by the time we stopped at the first street light, there was no doubt in my mind what I would be doing for the next several decades.

Billy had started talking about something or other, and again, I wasn't really listening because I was leaning over the railing staring into the fast-moving waters fifteen feet or so below. It was mesmerizing. I remember looking down the bridge line toward shore and watching the outgoing tide pouring out from between the spans, around the pilings, and wondering just how many bass would actually be there when the season got going in full swing. My brain was cranking.

And then I saw the rocks. My short little reverie on the bridge had just hit its first snag. From the top of the bridge, right where you walk on to the walkway, all the way down to the water's edge, was a steep slope of large craggy rocks, like break your neck, crack your skull type of terrain. To make matters worse, the only access to it was over the chain link fence, because the base of the bridge where the railing started, was too big a drop to the rocks, to simply jump from. I interrupted Billy mid-sentence.

"How the hell do you land a freak'in fish?"

Billy stopped and looked at me.

"Haven't you heard a word I been saying?"

"Umm, no…sorry."

"I've been explaining it to you for like the past minute…"

So after a little ball busting, Billy explained the process of landing a fish on the 2nd Wantagh bridge. Talk about intimidating. First you fight the fish until it's fairly tired and then you start walking it down toward the bank, passing your rod around the outside of the light poles as you come to them. Then as you get near the bank, you put your reel in free spool and thumb the reel enough to let the fish take line, while you race down toward the chain link fence, keeping tension on the line with your thumb, all the while. When you get to the chain link fence, you put the reel back in gear, take in any slack, and one hand, hop over the chain link fence, while holding your rod with the other. From there you start cranking back line while working your way down the rocks, in effect, fighting the fish as you go. The idea was to get to the bottom as quickly as you could and finish the fight there. Easy peasy, right? Billy assured me that I would be able to figure out the best way down the rocks soon enough, and once I was used to it, it would be like going down stairs. I looked at the rocks again and I wasn't so sure.

Billy and I then walked out to the little square concrete island, the south side of the boat channel, and I looked around. Directly opposite us, on the northern side of the boat channel, stood the bridge operator's tower. Rising out of the water into the night sky, shrouded in the light fog that was on the bay that night, it looked like some ancient castle fortress. Billy looked down the parkway, saw no headlights, and hopped over the concrete barriers onto the parkway and started walking over the drawbridge toward the operator's tower. I followed suit. When we got to the other side of the tower, we hopped the barriers again on to a walkway identical to the southside. We started walking toward the shore. As I looked down the bridge to shore, I couldn't help noticing, with some degree of dread, that the same steep slope of rocks existed on this side also. I'm sure Billy explained some stuff to me as we walked, but I really have no recollection of it, as my mind was way too busy trying to process this whole new fishing paradigm I was being introduced to. We crossed the parkway to east side, walked the bike path, climbed the chain link fence to look down into the shadow line, the shore and the bay, and then completed our cycle.

Next up was the 3rd Wantagh bridge, the southern-most on the Wantagh parkway. Again, I drove over the bridge and pulled over on a grassy area just past the bridge. Like the 2nd Wantagh, this bridge also had the same waist high chain link fence, joined at the base of the bridge to the exact same heavy steel pipe railing, and the same steep rock slopes going down to the water's edge. The difference here was that the 3rd Wantagh was not a drawbridge, therefor there was no protective walkway. Instead, you had about a six-foot section of pavement between the railing and the yellow line that marked the edge of right lane of the parkway, that you fished from. Cars would go whizzing by at sixty miles per hour, six feet from your butt!

It was on this bridge that I finally got to use my rod for the first time. After walking out onto the bridge for a bit, we stopped between two spans. Billy unhooked the bucktail from his rod and told me to watch what he did. The not so short version is that he swung the bucktail straight out in front of him, lifted his thumb off the spool to let out more line, then when the bucktail started to drop, he thumbed the spool and lifted, then dropped his rod which accelerated the big downward arc of the bucktail as it swung back under the bridge. At precisely the right moment he lifted his thumb off the spool, in effect, casting backwards up under the bridge until the bucktail touched down, which at the time I was sure required the possession of some alien sixth sense. He then thumbed the spool, put the reel in gear, lowered his rod, and waited for the bucktail to reach bottom, whereby he raised the rod tip sharply, and started taking in line just enough to keep the bucktail running along the bottom contour. When the bucktail came out from underneath the bridge, Billy put his reel in free spool and dropped his bucktail downtide until it bumped the bottom. At that point he thumbed the spool for a second or two while slowly lifting the rod, before going back into free spool again and repeating the process a couple more times. He then reeled in and told me to give it a try. Oh joy, I thought.

The Smiling Bill bucktail I had tied on earlier in the evening leered at me as I reached to unhook it from my rod guide.

"C'mon man, you got this!" it said mockingly. "You're a wiz with conventional gear, just go for it!"

I unhooked the 2-ounce bucktail, walked to the rail and dropped it over the side, thumbed the spool, and put my reel in free spool. I let the bucktail swing back and forth a couple times trying to get the feel and rhythm before making the initial cast out in front of me. When the bucktail had swung back to me, I dropped my rod tip some, and then lifted it sharply to get the bucktail moving forward quickly in an outward arc. When it reached the outer most point of the arc, I lifted my finger off the spool and let line flow off my reel, casting the bucktail straight out from my position. So far so good, I thought. After the bucktail traveled about six feet or so, I thumbed the reel to stop the forward progress of the bucktail and begin the downward arc that would carry the bucktail under the bridge for the next phase of the cast.

I remember Billy lifting his rod and then dropping it to accelerate the arc of the bucktail under the bridge, so I reared back on my rod and then dropped my rod tip. A second later I both heard, and saw my bucktail smack into the concrete of the bridge at my feet. Obviously, something was off with my technique, and as I reeled in my bucktail, Billy explained where I went wrong. My second attempt went better. I swung the bucktail out higher and farther, and waited longer before lifting and dropping the rod for acceleration. I even managed to free spool my reel at the end of the arc under the bridge sending my bucktail further back under the bridge. But I booted the bucktail landing and my reel started to bird nest. I quickly thumbed the reel and started stripping the thirty pound mono line off as fast as I could. I cleared the tangle in a matter of seconds, threw the reel in gear, and frantically started cranking in the cleared line. But by the time I got all the line back on the reel, it was too late, the bucktail had hit bottom, some twenty feet below, and been dragged along aided by the current, until it found a prime piece of structure to snag on to. My line came tight, but I couldn't free the bucktail. It was dug in like a Carolina tick.

Billy came over, took my rod and showed me something that I would wind up using on these bridges many times over the years. He let out enough line so that he could wrap it around the butt of my rod four or five times. He then stuck the butt side of my rod over the side of the bridge railing far enough so that the line would not rub against the concrete of the bridge base, and started walking down the bridge, applying increasing pressure to the snag as he walked. He kept walking and applying pressure, the object of the exercise being that eventually either the thirty pound mono would break, or the snag would free itself. After a few more steps, the line snapped and it was official, I had sacrificed my first bucktail to the 3rd Wantagh bridge.

Billy handed my rod back to me and as I was reeling in my slack line, he must have known what I was thinking, because he said something to me that clarified my thoughts and cemented my resolve on the spot.

"It's not quite what you thought it would be like is it?"

"Um, no. Not really," I said.

"Well, it's this simple. If you want to cash in on the riches these bridges have to offer, then there's a price you're gonna pay. The question is, are you willing to pay that price, because if it were that easy, everyone would be doing it, right?"

I just nodded my head.

He asked, "So, do you want to see more, or have you had enough?"

Without any hesitation, I said, "Lead on."

We quickly completed my tour of the 3rd Wantagh Bridge and returned to my car. Billy told me to drive the short distance to the Jones Beach needle, then head west on Ocean Parkway, which basically runs straight through Jones Beach State Park, before it bears right, and becomes the Meadowbrook Parkway, right at the base of the Big M Bridge. As I was slowly driving west through the state park, making sure I didn't get a speeding ticket in my excitement, I could see the Big M Bridge looming up out of the bay in the distance. Etched against the night sky, I was struck by her size and I immediately understood how she got her name. She was at least twice the length of any of the other bridges we had visited that night, and being a drawbridge, higher toward the center spans where the draw sections meet. From my point of view on the parkway, the street lights at the center section looked fuzzy and indistinct, almost ghostly, lost in the low ceiling of fog that had settled in on the bay.

As I rounded the turn heading onto the bridge, Billy told me to drive over the bridge and to continue driving over the following bridge, which was the Fundy Bridge. He said to stay in the left lane, because after the Fundy Bridge there would be a center area turn around, where we could pull in and head back the way we came. I did as instructed, and a few minutes later we were crossing back over the Big M. Billy told me that as soon as we finished crossing, to pull over onto the paved area of the shoulder where the bridge operator parks. I remember thinking to myself *Gee, this is convenient, what happens if the bridge operator shows up?*

Billy, who had already developed an uncanny knack for picking off my thoughts said, "Don't worry about the bridge operator, they never open this bridge anymore. Besides, I know the guy."

I almost started to laugh out loud.

Billy looked at me and said, "What?"

I just shook my head and smiled.

The tide was still outgoing, so we grabbed our rods and crossed to the southeast side of the bridge. Back then, the Big M had walkways on both sides of the bridge. On the west side, where we had parked, the walkway had a three-rail steel railing on the water side, and a two-rail steel railing on the parkway side. The east side had the same thing except for one little addition. That addition was that the concrete of the walkway extended approximately eighteen inches or so beyond, or outside, where the water side, three-rail steel railing was anchored, creating a ledge. Billy and I started walking out on the southeast side walkway with Billy in the lead, as usual. As we walked, we noticed that there was a boat anchored uptide of the shadow line. When we got closer, we saw that he had a couple of rods out and figured he was fishing bait, as his mono lines were clearly visible due to their reflections from the street lights on the bridge.

We stopped a little way past where the boat was fishing and without saying a word, Billy nonchalantly climbed over the water side railing and out onto the eighteen inch ledge. He unhooked his bucktail, took up a little slack, and then proceeded to start walking along the ledge, back the way we came, while looking down into the shadow line the street lights were casting on the water below. His rod was in his left hand and his right hand would barely make contact with the railing, like some absent-minded, unnecessary motion. Back then we both smoked, so while he was still walking, he took his right hand, put it in his pocket, pulled out his cigarettes, got one out, lit it, put everything back in his pocket, twenty-five feet above the middle of Sloop Channel, like he was just out walking the dog in the park!

He looked back at me and said, "What are you waiting for?"

Now, my motto in life has always been that I would try almost anything once, and it has gotten me into some pretty f'd up situations at times, and I was wondering right then and there, if this was about to be another one of those times. Like a neon sign, a thought started flashing in my brain, *This is only bridge number four, it can't get any weirder than this, can it?* So I propped my rod up on the other side of the railing, and slowly climbed over, clinging for dear life to the top railing the whole time. Once I managed to get my feet planted and get vertical, my right hand was squeezing the top railing so tight, my knuckles were white. I picked up my rod and started making my way down, with baby steps, toward Billy.

As I got closer to Billy, I could see the smile beneath his bushy Horseshoe mustache, and the twinkle in his eyes reflecting the street lights, as he casually stood there waiting for me.

"You're supposed to be looking down into the shadow line," he said.

"Um…yeah, I haven't quite gotten that far yet, you know?"

"Well the railing's not going anywhere, so why don't you give it a try."

I figured, in for a penny, in for a pound, so with my right hand gripping the top rail I looked down into the abyss. I guess the damage from the serious ear infections I had experienced several years earlier had started to have an effect on my balance, because the sudden body rush feeling of falling over the side caused me to pull back suddenly.

"WHOA!"

I took a deep breath and looked at Billy. The smile was still there and he didn't look surprised in the least.

"That happens to everybody the first time," he said.

"Did it happen to you?" I asked.

"No."

Figures I thought sarcastically.

He said, "Try it again, but this time don't think about the height so much, just relax, go slow, concentrate on the shadow line and look for fish. Think about the fish, not about the height, you're not going to fall."

I laughed a little bit. "Yeah, if you say so."

Billy put his right hand out and made that universal calm down, relax gesture.

"You'll be fine, just takes a bit of getting used to."

So I took another breath and looked out at the bay for a short bit, then moved my eyes toward where the anchored boat was, and then gradually moved them onto the shadow line bringing them back up toward me until they were looking down at the shadow line beneath me. I waited for the body rush, but it didn't come, which was truly a relief. I remember standing there on that ledge, looking down into the black moving water and thinking: *What a really cool thing to be doing in the middle of the night, scary as hell, but really cool.* My thoughts were interrupted by Billy.

"You OK?"

"Yeah," I said. "I think I'm good."

"Well then, are you ready to take a little walk?" he asked.

"I guess so, just don't go too fast."

He turned and we started walking toward the anchored boat while scanning the shadow line below for fish. We only went about fifteen feet or so to the next light before Billy stopped.

"Check out the size of those Needlefish," he said, and he pointed down into the shadow line.

I edged up closer to him and followed his point down. Sure enough, I could see the two Needlefish he was talking about darting out from the dark shadow line, picking off the unsuspecting baitfish that were drawn in by the light of the street lamp.

Billy told me to back up a little as he got into position to make a cast.

"I'm going to see if I can get one to hit my bucktail," he said. "Watch where I cast and how I bring the bucktail across the shadow line at an angle in front of them."

Standing on that little ledge, without the slightest fear of falling, he lob casted the bucktail about forty-five degrees to his right, toward the boat, which we were quite close to at that point. It landed about twelve feet or so outside the shadow line. Billy quickly engaged the reel and started reeling the bucktail just below the surface

41

toward the shadow line. Even at that height, I could clearly see the bucktail and white Uncle Josh pork rind fluttering behind it. Just as it neared the shadow line, one of the Needle fish darted out and took a stab at the bucktail, but missed the hook, which was a bit too big for them anyway. Billy just chuckled and reeled in his line.

It was about that time that one of the guys in the boat decided to join the party.

"Hey man! I don't like you casting so close to my boat, we got lines out!"

Billy waved him off. "Ah don't worry about it, I'm not going to hit your boat, or your lines, not even close."

"Well, we're trying to fish down here you know!"

"I see that, and trying is all you'll be doing," Billy quipped. "If there were any fish on this bridge, I would have seen'em already."

Billy turned to me and said, "Let's go."

He climbed the railing back onto the walkway and I did the same. I could hear the guy in the boat shouting obscenities from down below and I started laughing, not only because I found it funny, but more so as a cathartic release of nerves. We jumped the highway side railing, crossed the parkway, jumped the concrete divider, waited for a car to go whizzing by, and ran to the west side. We hopped the highway railing and took a tour of the west side of the bridge. This side resembled a bigger version of the 2nd Wantagh Bridge, but as Billy explained, the Big M was mostly sand bottom so snags were not an issue. I also remember him saying that this was one of the few bridges that produced well on both sides of the tide and being closer to the inlet, had produced many big fish for him. After those key points, it was time to move on.

We jumped back in my car, got headed north on the Meadowbrook Parkway, courtesy of the nearby Bay Parkway cloverleaf, over the Big M, across Jones Island, and when we crossed the Fundy Bridge, I pulled off to the grassy shoulder just past the bridge. Having driven over this bridge twice now, I kind of knew what to expect, and I wasn't going to like it. We got out, but left our rods, and walked toward the bridge. The Fundy Bridge was kind of a miniature version of the 3rd Wantagh Bridge without the chain link fence. It was smaller in length, with only two street lights, but had the same rock sides that descended down to the water's edge, that would need to be negotiated when landing a fish.

But the worst part was that instead of having a six foot section of pavement between you, and the solid white line marking the edge of the right lane, to fish from, on this bridge you had at best two feet. That meant that while you were bent over fighting a fish, a passenger in a car could tap you on your back while driving by! That's a nice way of saying that a little swerve to the right in the middle of the night, and you were road kill. The good news was that like the Big M, the Fundy Bridge was sand bottom with no real snags to speak of. Billy was busy checking out all the bait in the water, but at my suggestion, we didn't stick around.

On the road again, I jumped into the left lane and into the center turn-around area, where I U-turned and headed back south over the Fundy Bridge. Just past the bridge, Billy told me bear right onto the Loop Parkway exit, but that before I completed the turn I should pull off onto the grass where a dirt road led behind a row of bushes that ran parallel to the exit road. It came up quick, and in the dark I almost missed it, but managed to pull it off at the last second. *Nice hiding spot* I thought to myself, *I wonder if I'm going to get covered in ticks.*

After parking a little way up the dirt road, we got out, grabbed our rods and walked back down the dirt road to the base of the Swift Creek Bridge. We walked out on the north side of the bridge, which again, reminded me a lot of the 3rd Wantagh Bridge. The north side of the bridge had two street lights, and a three-rail railing along the water side of the bridge. And while it didn't have the six foot space between the railing and the white line border of the right lane, it did have somewhere between four and five feet of space, which after the Fundy Bridge, seemed like a mile. The south side of the bridge had NO space between the railing and the white line border of the right lane, therefore, I had NO interest in that side of the bridge.

We stopped just past the first street light to take some casts. Being on the south side of the Swift Creek bridge meant that the outgoing tide had the current running toward us and under the bridge, just like it was at the Big M, so the elaborate under the bridge, swing cast technique was not used here. Basically, the plan was you either spotted fish in the shadow line and swam your

44

bucktail in front of them at an angle, or you blind casted your bucktail further out at an angle, let it hit bottom, and bounced it back to you through the shadow line and underneath the bridge. This was the first time I got to experience casting in this manner from up top of a bridge and to be honest, I found it a bit of a let-down. As I was already fully competent with conventional gear, the casting was easy, the bottom was sandy and snag free, and the current was sluggish. Compared to everything else I had experienced earlier, this bridge was decidedly ho-hum. Billy asked if I wanted to check out the other side. I said I'd take a pass and that I wanted to move on.

After backing out of the dirt road, a quick hop west over Meadow Island brought us to the Loop Parkway Bridge. Just before the bridge, I pulled off to the right onto a paved area in front of a small utility building. The Loop Parkway Bridge is a draw bridge with a walkway on the south side of the bridge that leads out to the bridge operator's building. It had the same railing configuration as the Big M Bridge, three-rail railing to the water's side, two-rail railing on the traffic side. The north side of the bridge did not have a walkway, but did have the three-rail railing with the eighteen inch ledge on its outer side. And both sides of the bridge had a feature unique to draw bridges.

On each side of the bridge, there are square concrete platforms that hold the vehicle gates, which come down to stop traffic prior to the draw bridge raising. Billy explained that these platforms have the railing running around them and make a good place to fish under one condition. When the bells went off, you needed to make sure you got your ass to the side rails and out of the way of the counter weight coming up and the back rail, otherwise you were going swimming with broken legs. The warning was duly noted and stored away for future reference.

We had walked out on the south side of the bridge, on the bridge operator's walkway, out to about the second light. The Loop Parkway Bridge is directly in line with Jones Inlet, and we stood there for a while, looking out at the dark inlet, watching the lights from boats coming in and going out. The warm August southerlies were heavy with the smell of salt, fresh off the ocean, a fragrance I knew I could never get tired of. Billy gave me more information about the bridge, how it produced on both tides, was good late in the season, other useful bits of info, but at that point my available RAM had been exceeded, my tea cup was full, and I was done.

We took a quick trip down to the Point Lookout Bridge simply because we had to go there to turn around, in order to head home. While we were there, I pulled over and we got out and looked down the bridge. We didn't even walk out on it. Billy said a few things which I didn't remember and we headed back toward the Dunkin' Donuts. While we originally came up via the Wantagh Parkway, going back we went north on the Meadowbrook Parkway down toward Merrick Road. I was asking Billy a few questions about this and that, and a short while after crossing the Fundy Bridge, Billy interrupted me mid-sentence.

"That was the 1st Meadowbrook Bridge," he said.
"What?"

"That was the 1st Meadowbrook Bridge we just crossed over back there."

"Where?" I asked, "I didn't even see it!"

"Not surprised," he said, "It's not much and not very well lit, just one street light, so don't worry, you didn't miss anything. It's pretty much a boat spot."

I took his word for it and about ten minutes later we were ordering coffee and some donuts at the D&D. As we sat there, Billy explained that fishing from the bridges was illegal, so it was not uncommon to get chased off by the State Police. They will drive by with their bull horns on and tell us to get off the bridge. When that happens, he said he usually comes here, gets a cup of coffee and a donut, waits for about an hour, and then goes back fishing. He went on to say that sometimes the State Troopers would even give out summonses for fishing on the bridge, you just never knew. I would learn first-hand how nasty enforcement could get after 09/11/2001. He also said the D&D was a good place to wait out a tide change, and we finished the evening talking about his early days of bridge fishing.

Very few pictures of me from back in the day. I found this one taken by my wife, before she was my wife. She asked me what I fished for at night, so I showed her. No idea of the weight.

Bridging The Gap…

When Billy and I decided to do this book, it quickly became apparent that there was no way in hell that I would be able to remember everything that we talked about, let alone commit it to print. There also appeared to be no definitive way to organize the stories, simply because we both lacked the discipline to stay on one topic for very long. We'd agree to talk about a certain topic and that would last about three minutes before we were off to the races, "Oh, do you remember when…" So far, the story has been roughly split between how I met Billy and was introduced to fishing the west end bridges, and a transcribed conversation of Billy's early years with Frank Dominic. So what now? I've set the stage, so how do I fill the spaces, make the transition, sync everything up, and tell some stories?

Well, the first thing I realized was that I would need to record all of our conversations. The recordings took care of the memory issue and resulted in many, many hours of dialogue, stories and specifics. This resulted in a bunch of different audio files that sometimes became difficult to keep track of. But later on, during the book-writing planning stage, I got bogged down trying to figure out how I would write out these conversations and stories, not necessarily from my perspective, but from Billy's. I played around with it for a while, but I just couldn't make any of it sound like the reader was listening to two guys talking. It kept coming up like formatted novel dialog. I couldn't catch the immediateness of the moment, the feeling of being in the room, so to speak, no matter how I tried. Finally we said screw it, and made the decision to simply transcribe our conversations and stories. The recordings not only preserved our conversations, stories, and little details for transcription, they also allowed me to capture Billy's cadence of speech and sense of humor, in the most accurate manner possible.

The second thing, or problem really, was our aforementioned inability to stay on topic for very long. One thing reminds you of another, and another, you just can't help it, so while my various recordings have file names that are supposed to indicate what the contents are, they only kind of, maybe, sometimes, do so in the beginning. Because of this, I've had to go through endless hours of audio in order to cherry pick various conversations and stories, in an attempt to assemble them into some logical sequence. While from this point forward, we're going to try and follow some sort of chronological road map, expect some bumps and detours along the way. So, let's start back where it all began.

Rich: I know you saw some guy fishing from the top of the Big M when you were fishing with Frank Dominic back in the day, and that that is how you got introduced to bridge fishing. What was that all about?

Billy: Yeah, Frank and I were clam chumming the bridge, and I saw this guy walking a fish down. Frank didn't know what he was doing because nobody really fished the bridges back then. But I knew that guy had a fish and I wanted to know what that was all about. I was like sixteen at the time, and I was already a really good fisherman by then, but I wanted to know about everything. [*laughs*]

Rich: So what happened?

Billy: What happened? What do you think happened? [*laughs*] I went up there. I'd ride my bike down there at night and go out on the bridge. I'd see the guy, but every time he sees me coming, he'd take off. He does this to me a couple times, so I figure he's gotta land a fish at some point, right? So one night I go down under the bridge, when I know he's up there fishing. He hooks up and I'm looking down the shadow line watching him walking his fish down. He gets closer, so I back up under the bridge and when he comes down to unhook it, I come out of the shadows behind him. Now he can't run away.

Rich: So what did he say?

Billy: He says, "OK kid, you got me. What do you want?" Being the kind of kid I was, you know, aggressive, no BS, I just came straight out and told him I wanted to catch fish like he did. He got quiet for a couple seconds, then he bends over, puts his hand on my shoulder, and looks me straight in the eyes, like he was measuring me up or something, you know. He says, "Can you keep a secret?" It felt like I was being initiated into some kind of secret society. [*laughs*] I told him I could and promised I would never tell anybody. He says, "Good, because if you can keep your mouth shut, you can have these fish all to yourself."

Rich: [*laughing*] The passing of the torch… and that's all it took, huh.

Billy: You bet. I'd ride my bike down there every night I wasn't fishing with Frank. I saw what that guy was doing. After that it didn't take me too long to figure out how it worked.

Rich: So, you just started walking along the ledge, casting bucktails to fish you spotted in the shadow line?

Billy: Yeah, pretty much. Well back then it was little different, like I could ride my bike out onto the bridge and nobody cared. Listen to this, this is funny. When I would bring a bass home for dinner, I would jam the handle bar through the gills, but the fish were so big, they would drag on the street. By the time I'd get home, the tails were burned off from dragging on the pavement. My mother thought this was funny and she was always telling the neighbors I brought home fish with no tails [*laughs*]... When I first started fishing the bridge, there were no cops or bay constables busting our balls, none of that, that came much later. There were only State Troopers, and only a few of them, and they didn't seem to care what we did. And we didn't fish bucktails back then either, we fished eel skins.

Rich: Eel skins… you mean like eel skin plugs?

Billy: No, these are completely different, they haven't been made in decades. I still have a few around, I should take a picture of one and send it to you. I had one on at the 3rd Wantagh one night, and you didn't even notice it.

Rich: Really? Are you bs'ing me?

Billy: No, I did! I practically slapped you in the face with it a couple times, but you didn't even notice it. I guess we were too busy catching fish [*laughs*]. Anyway… they're kind of like a bucktail head, a little different shape, more oval, with a hole that runs from the front to just under where the hook comes out, for water to come through. And instead of tying bucktail to the back, you tie the last four or five inches of an eel skin on instead. When you retrieve it, water comes through the hole and fills the eel skin, looks just like a real eel. I tell you what, those things really caught fish, but they'd get pretty skanky after a while.

Rich: I bet… I guess you were freezing them between uses.

Billy: Yeah, you had to… You know, two of the original guys who used to fish the bridges made a bait-tail lure that was based on those eel skins. It was pretty popular for a while, not sure if it's still around. You know the one I'm talking about right?

Rich: Yes I do… and you know I made all my own bait-tails back then, right. I still have hundreds of heads left. Hundreds… Sometime back in the late 90s, yeah, pretty sure it was around then, a fishing friend of mine who also crewed on sail boats, he got access to about 1,700 pounds of lead that was cut out of the hull of his friend's sailboat.

Billy: Wow, that's a lot, that's almost a ton!

Rich: Yup, piled up under a tree. We went over to the guy's house, loaded up several hundred pounds, which pretty much bottomed out my Blazer and his Jeep, and brought it back to my shop. I bought a big smelter, some molds, mostly spearhead jig heads for the bait-tails and vertical fishing stuff, some shad heads, bullet-nose, hot-lips, and a few other molds, and all the recommended hooks, and we dove right in. Turned out that the recommended hooks for the molds sucked, like they were total crap. I took some of the first batch of bait-tails I made to a spot I called Three-Rocks, on the back side of Moriches Inlet west… I never told you this story, about this spot, it's a great story, you gotta hear this one so don't interrupt me.

Billy: [laughs] I thought we were talking about me?

Rich: We were, but this is really good, you'll like it. It's a good story... You know how I'm framing part of the book on how much chance plays a part in our lives, right. Well, Three Rocks is a great example of this. In the 90s, in addition to the bridges at night, I also used to fish around Moriches Inlet during the day, night also... depended on the tides around the bridges... Anyway, I would park my Blazer right at the backside of Moriches Inlet west, as far back as you could, right before this little path that went down to the shore and back to an area that the guys who fished around there called the meadows. It was just a small sod bank. I fished the meadows a lot, it was a good spot, but I also had a few other spots in the area that I kept to myself.

Here's the luck part. One weekday, I had just come around the corner of my Blazer and had started walking toward the little path to go out to the meadows, when I almost bumped into two scuba divers who had come walking up the path. They were pretty amped up. The short version is they pointed down at the water, next to where we were standing, and told me that exactly where they were pointing, there were four or five huge bass, just laying behind three big rocks on the bottom. I'm standing there thinking *WTF,* I couldn't tell whether they were bs'ing me or not, but they kept babbling on about these fish. They looked for real, you know what I mean.

So they leave and I'm standing there wondering what to do. I only had spinning gear with me, 25 pound XL mono, which is what I fished the meadows with back then, so I wasn't really equipped to deal with the kind of water ripping through where they had pointed. But I put on a bucktail anyway. I'd never fished that little stretch before, I'd never seen anybody fish it really, so I had no idea what to expect. I waded out across ten feet or so of shallow water and bowling ball sized rocks before the bottom dropped straight down. I started lobbing casts up current, you know, trying to get a feel for where the bottom was, but the current was ripping and my bucktail was too light, so I couldn't feel anything. I wound up getting snagged. I gave it another shot, but got hung up again, so I said screw it and headed for the meadows.

But I couldn't get what those divers had told me out of my head, so I came back the next day with my bridge stick aka the Big Dog, and some three ounce sinkers. I made that spot one of my special projects, like I did the 3rd Wantagh bridge, you know. I learned every inch of that bottom like the back of my hand, and I did it in a hurry. I wanted to know if those jokers were pulling my leg or not. Turns out, there's a rock wall, kind of thing that you had to walk out to that runs east-west along there. It was pretty tricky because it was filled with the bowling ball sized rocks I mentioned before, and usually covered with a foot or so of moving water, so the footing was pretty sketchy. I'd guess the wall is like forty, or fifty feet long, and it must be man-made because its dead straight, and drops straight down, and I mean straight down. Turns out it's also a great blackfish spot.

Anyway, it's about ten feet deep at the east end and gets deeper as it goes to the west, toward the back of the jetty, to about sixteen or eighteen feet. The wall ends where it meets the back rock wall of the jetty. That wall is literally the edge of the boat channel, so the current rips through there, and it's pretty snaggy. The large rocks are down there, I'm assuming there are three of them like the divers said, but they are a little further west than where the divers originally had pointed, pretty much near the end of the wall, by where it meets the jetty. They're probably left-overs from building the jetty, but back then they held some really big fish, even in broad daylight. Fishing that wall always gave me the creeps. I was always worried it was going to give way with me on it.

I was thinking of those scuba guys the first time I caught a big fish off those rocks, and pulling big fish out of there was no joke, I tell you. It's like fishing the 2nd Wantagh from shore, you know, off the ridge at the 2nd span. Same kind of thing. At that point I had figured everything out, the weight of the bait-tail, where to drop the cast, the snags, the timing of the lift to clear the rocks, everything. That spot was mine, I owned it.

It was early October I think, and a lot of mullet were still leaving the bay. It's why I loved that area for daytime fishing at that time of year. The main boat channel swung right into shore by that area, the meadows, that I mentioned before, and the bass would be waiting for the mullet on the outgoing tide. This was right at the backside of the inlet, the mullet had no place to go, they had to pass through there. Back then, there were some epic daytime blitzes there. We had outgoing all afternoon and there was a good bite at the meadows, some good fish too. Tide slowed and the bite died, and the two guys who were there left to go out front. I ran back to my Blazer and grabbed the Big Dog and got out on the ledge. I was already rigged and on my second pass over the top of the rocks I got smacked.

I immediately leaned on her to death and got her to move out from the rocks, and I just kept` leaning and little cranks and she gave some. You know my rod and how I fish, either the rod breaks, or the fifty pound Ande snaps, but I'm not letting her get her head turned. I got her in pretty quick. She was about thirty pounds. I slid her up on the ledge, which still had about six or eight inches of water on it, and she soaked the crap out of me with her tail slapping. So… I guess I can chalk that spot up to my chance meeting with those two scuba guys and they get sole credit for the spot's name of *Three Rocks*.

Billy: That's a nice story.

Rich: Actually, I'm not done yet [*laughing*] So what was I talking about… oh yeah, the recommended hooks for the molds, those pieces of crap. I was so psyched to be able to crank out an unlimited supply of bait-tails. I ran out to Moriches to test out some of my first batch. I had a two-ounce bait-tail on the Big Dog, got out on the ledge to fish Three Rocks and hooked up right away. I leaned hard on the fish and in no time, like ten seconds, that fish was gone. I reeled in a safety pin instead of a hook, it bent right out, complete crap. I was suspicious of them to begin with, but I didn't think they were that weak. Fortunately, we didn't make that many heads. We threw them all back into the smelter.

So I modified the crap out of those molds to take brass eyes and really heavy J-hooks, I mean really heavy wire J-hooks, not bucktail hooks. You could tow a car with these things. Years ago, in its infancy, a now popular online surf fishing magazine that I occasionally write for, you know the name, they did a video of me pouring my heads and the modifications I had done to the molds. I doubt the video is still out there though. With making the bait-tails, the real bitch was buying surgical tubing for the tails. [*laughs*] Surgical supply houses wouldn't sell it to me, they thought I was a drug addict and I wanted it for tying myself off. [*laughing*] I still have a bunch of heads and creations that I'll never use down here. You want some? I'll send you some if you want.

Billy: Sure, I'll take'em.

Rich: Your first fifty came off the Big M right?

Billy: No, I actually caught my first fifty from a boat, with Frank. We were fishing live bait off the Rockaways. Those jetties held a ton of big fish. There were days we would fill the boat with thirty to fifty pound fish, and nobody was doing that back then. Nobody.

Rich: So when did you catch your first fifty from a bridge?

Billy: That first fifty was caught on the Meadowbrook Bridge, it was like 1971, late October on the moon. You know… I was thinking about it coming home, when we were talking before, and it's like you're trying to remember all the conditions, but man, I had so many times on the bridge. I remember the fish, I remember where I caught'em, but I couldn't tell you everything about it, but I can tell you a lot. It was on a new moon, listen, that's the fish that did it for me, I mean we always knew the moons were better, the older guys would always tell you that, but you get a big fish on a moon, it really clicks, you know what I mean, and that was a new moon, and I remember that clear as a bell.

I had been fishing the bridge whenever I wasn't fishing with Frank, there were a lot of big fish around back then. My sister had this little Volkswagen Bug, she used to let me take it at night, I was like seventeen at the time I think, yeah seventeen, I think I had my license then. [*laughs*] So I took it over to the bridge, I'd say it was somewhere

60

around eleven o'clock. Nobody was on the bridge. I walked out and I see this fish, right under the light, he was right up on top, like his back was practically out of the water, you couldn't miss him. I could tell right away it was a really big fish, and I got that big adrenaline rush, like all my senses went on high alert. By then I'd caught enough good fish from the bridge, to know what to do, but nothing this big, so I was really excited, but focused, you know what I mean.

I got that fish on the first cast. I swam that eel skin right into his mouth and he ate it! That fish blew under the bridge so fast, I couldn't believe it. I wasn't ready for that, before I could even blink my rod smacks up against bridge. I was panicking a little bit, you know. No matter how good a fisherman you are, when you first start fishing the bridges, there's always a little bit of luck to get some of these fish in. As you get older, it becomes more skill because you know what's going to happen, but a little luck doesn't hurt either. Big fish don't go quietly.

But I was really struggling with this fish to get him out from under the bridge, I mean this fish had me on my hands and knees. Back then I was still using forty pound test on a Squidder. I hadn't graduated to fifty pound mono yet, so I didn't know how hard I could lean on him. I was really sweating it. On a boat, you can let a big fish run a little bit, you know, there's nothing for him to cut you off on, but you can't do that on the bridge or he'll saw you off on the pilings, so I was just hanging on, hoping the forty pound test wouldn't snap, and man, I

61

wanted that fish so bad! I really did. I had to fight off the adrenaline and not do something stupid, you know, stay patient. It took me a while, but I finally got that fish out from under the bridge. I worked him down to the end of the bridge, free-spooled the reel, sprinted to the end of, and around the walkway, threw the reel in gear and went down the side as fast as I could go, cranking all the way. I got him in, stuck my thumb into his jaw, clamped down, and pulled his ass up onto the rocks. Man, my heart was pounding! [*laughing*]

Rich: Then what?

Billy: Then what? Then I threw him in the car and drove down to Frank's to weigh'em in… and how stupid was that? [*laughs*] I mean if I was older I would have stayed all night looking for another big one, but I was so excited, I left with him. [*laughing*]

Rich: You what?

Billy: I left! I knew it was a really, really, big fish, you know what I mean… I blew it, I took the fish, threw it in the car, and left. [*laughing*] I didn't know how big he was, but I knew it was a really big fish. I was so excited I wanted to weigh it in as fast as I could, and I got home and I realized that Frank's was closed until the morning, when I got there for work… Turns out he was fifty-three pounds. But that's what you do when you're a kid. [*laughs*] Like now, sometimes I go to the beach and I see a guy get a big fish, not even a real big fish, like a thirty pound fish, he runs off the beach, the sinker's dragging in the sand, the hook's still in the fish's mouth, and he's running to his car, and I say to myself, we probably all did that at one point! [*laughing*]

Rich: So I'm guessing that pretty much marked the beginning of your quest for big fish from the bridges.

Billy: You know, I never really thought of it that way. When I first started fishing the bridges, it wasn't to catch big fish, I'd already caught plenty of big fish from the boat with Frank. I was still pin hooking with Frank during the day, but that was mostly small, market fish, but at night I'd go up on the bridges, and that was a whole different thing. There was something about fishing the bridges at night that was almost magical, or mystical, you know what I mean. I'm not sure exactly how to describe it, but you know what I'm talking about, I saw it in your eyes the first time I took you up there. It either grabs you and gets inside of you or it doesn't. It's that simple.

But here's the thing, and I learned this very early on, is that when I was fishing from up top I could see fish in the shadow line. Yeah, there were plenty of fish on the bottom also, but there would be fish feeding on the surface, with their noses right up at the shadow line, and I could see those fish. I've always had great vision, so I could see these fish plain as day, so this allowed me to be able to target really big fish. When you're fishing from a boat or the surf, you can't see the fish. You might know that there are big fish around, but you're still depending on luck to bring that big fish to your bait. But on top of a bridge, I can target big fish because I can *see* them.

Once I knew those big fish were there, I just had to learn how to catch them. Some of the stuff was obvious you know, but some things you just don't think about when you're young. I'd spot a good fish, and get that shot of adrenaline, you know, and I'd get over to him and he'd drop out of the shadow line. I kept wondering why sometimes that would happen, and then it hit me. It was my shadow!... The street lights cast your shadow down on the water in different places depending on where you are on the bridge, and it just didn't occur to me at first! But I figured it out soon enough.

Then I had to learn how to make the perfect cast to those fish. There's a lot that goes into making a cast to fish that are feeding in the shadow line. You got to be in the right spot on the bridge, you have to figure how far in front of the shadow line to make the cast, the current speed, the angle, your retrieve speed, you got to bring it right to him, right across his nose. If you blow it on the first cast, you can forget about catching that fish, he won't touch it after that. The cast is the single most important thing where catching those big fish is concerned. Every big fish I've ever caught, I've caught on the first cast, every single one.

Here's the other thing. I was already an accomplished fisherman at an early age, but nobody remembers guys who catch a lot of bass, but people will always remember your name if you catch really big bass. So I quickly started to develop a reputation as someone who caught monster bass because I was able to target those big fish from the bridges. So yeah, I guess you could say that catching that first fifty on the Meadowbrook kind of got me pointed in that direction.

Rich: I guess it also got you to move up to fifty pound test pretty quick. [*laughs*]

Billy: Actually, I couldn't tell you the date, but I'm pretty sure it was right after the next time I snapped off a big fish [*laughing*]. That sound will make you throw up… it's like a gunshot going off under the bridge. Losing a big fish is the worst feeling in the world, it sticks with you for quite a while, you know. Look, you use something until it doesn't work anymore, then you try something else. Forty wasn't working for me. I couldn't let these fish run around under the bridge, so I had to move up to fifty. I'd have gone straight to eighty if I could have gotten enough line on the reel. [*laughs*]

Rich: You know, I've known you for decades but I really don't know much about your earlier years. I mean, I know the basics, like the stuff that was in your book, and other stuff you've mentioned, but not a lot of the bridge fishing stuff, the stuff that was in your head at the time. So, how did your whole bridge thing come together back then, I mean you started cranking out a steady stream of big fish and I know that didn't happen just by chance.

Billy: Your right, it wasn't luck. [*laughs*] Look, you and me, we're both very analytical and methodical in the way we do things right?... Well, I was that way when I was young also. I had nine bridges, all within a five minute drive of each other, and I fished every one of them, every single one, all the time. You know how it goes, there are years where there's only a pick of big fish, and then there are years where the bridges are loaded with them.

So I got into my routine of going from bridge, to bridge, to bridge and then I stayed on one bridge and fished. I'd start at the Point Lookout, then the Loop, the Swift Creek, the Fundy, the Meadowbrook, 3rd Wantagh, 2nd Wantagh, you know what I mean. And I didn't fish... I would walk right across the bridge, and if I didn't see something four feet long, I'd go right to the next bridge, because I'm looking for them big fish. That's the main reason I caught way more big fish than everybody else, because I was looking for real big fish. And if the front bridges didn't have any big fish, I would wind up at the 3rd Wantagh and just have fun catching fish. The 3rd Wantagh always had the most fish by far of any of the other bridges, and some big fish too at times.

And then there were weeks when there were a ton of big fish around. Listen, I had a week on the Meadowbrook where I probably had eight fish over fifty... this is off the top of my head of course, but that's what could happen

66

sometimes. Back then, not a lot of people fished bridges, and they didn't go every night. I fished every night. I didn't care if it was raining or snowing, you had to be there when the big fish showed up. You've seen this, I've had nights where I walked the south side of the bridge and there's nothing there, I get to the north side and there's twenty-five fish in the line. That kind of thing happened all the time back then. And one of the best bridges for really big fish years ago was the Swift Creek Bridge.

Rich: The Swift? Really?

Billy: Yeah! Nobody fished that bridge.

Rich: I didn't either. [*laughs*]

Billy: I had a ton of big fish on that bridge and nobody fished that bridge.

Rich: Weird… You know, I fished there off and on, because I liked the parking, and this might sound strange, but the fish I caught there were just average, cookie cutter fish.

Billy: If you told me that I'm going to tell you that you were fishing the outgoing tide.

Rich: Yeah, I was.

Billy: Yeah, because all the big fish are one hundred percent on incoming.

Rich: Ah! See, I fished the outgoing, the tide always seemed slow moving, sand bottom, no snags, after going through all the trouble to learn the Wantaghs, this just didn't seem like a fish bridge to me.

Billy: [*laughs*] The Swift was a little nothing bridge that no one really paid attention to, but I had fished it in the boat a lot, and there was a deep cut on the south side that came off the second span, and those big fish sat there religiously, you know. There were some huge fish there at times.

Rich: Geez, I wish I would have known about that!

Billy: You should've asked, I would've told you.

Rich: [*laughing*] Yeah, right.

Billy: [*laughing*]

Rich: Well, even if you did, I'm not sure I would have fished that side. I mean as scary as the Fundy is, the south side of the Swift is just plain nuts... you're literally standing in the right lane, there's not even a little strip of white line to squeeze behind. You could be bent over trying to pull a fifty out from under the bridge and some car could pull up, and the passenger could roll down his window and snatch your wallet right out of your back pocket and take off before you even knew what happened!

Billy: [*laughing*] Yeah, he could have!

Rich: You know, sometimes I think you must have had an angel on your shoulder all those years, because you had no fear of anything, and you've dodged everything. I mean… I know you have great balance and all and walking the ledge on the Big M, before they re-did it, was no big deal to you, but a couple of the bridges, like the Fundy, and Point Lookout, the north side of the Loop, the east side of the Meadowbrook, all they have is a foot or two between the white line and the railing. I was never comfortable fishing them. I just had trouble concentrating with cars whizzing by two feet away from me. I would usually only fish them if I couldn't find fish on any of the other bridges, or late at night, when there weren't that many cars on the road. But I always worried about drunk drivers. But you, you've fished them hard for decades, walking around on them like you have some sort of invisible shield around you that cars would bounce off of, or something. I got to hand it to you, you got some set of balls.

Billy: [*laughs*]

I'll Just Rest My Eyes For A Second...

Billy: I had been on a tremendous bite of big fish for a while. Every night on the Meadowbrook there were big fish popping up and I just couldn't stop fishing. The tides were getting later and later each night and I was just fishing and then going to work, and I was exhausted, but it was late in the season, you know, so they could be leaving any minute. So I'm out there on the Meadowbrook, on the east side, this is before they rebuilt it, when the little ledge was still there. And I'm walking along the ledge looking for a fish, and my eyes are just burning, like completely dry, and it's like three in the morning, and I'm shot. And I think, I just need to close my eyes for a second. So I sit down on the ledge with my legs hanging over the side of the bridge, lay my rod down on the ledge, and wrap my arm around the railing post and middle rail, lay my head there, and close my eyes. When I opened my eyes, the sun was up, it was after seven o'clock! I slept for like four hours with my legs dangling over the bridge!

Rich: Oh sh!t!

Billy: When I first opened my eyes, I thought for a second I was home in my bed, you know, and then I look down and see the water. I couldn't believe I didn't fall off the bridge! I mean, how stupid...

Rich: You know, I can easily think of a half dozen endings to this story, and they all end up with you in the water. No offense Bro.

Billy: None taken. [laughing]

Rich: You know, years ago I had a friend that lived out on Long Beach, a guy I knew from my days at Nor'east. Cindy and I went out there one night for his son's birthday party. After the party we hung out for a while and when we left, it was probably around midnight. As I'm getting ready to make the left to go over The Point Lookout Bridge, I mentioned that I wondered if anybody was fishing the bridge. Cindy is like, what do mean, and I tell her that these are some of the bridges I fish when I go out at night. So the light turned, and we're going over the bridge, and without thinking I pointed out which street light I liked to fish near and Cindy freaked out. She never realized that when I fished a bridge, that most times I was actually standing on top of the bridge, squeezed up against the railing of the right lane.

Now, you know Cindy has never, ever interfered with my fishing in any way. She knew what she was getting when we got married, and she's been great all these years, but the next day she told me she was not too happy about the idea of me fishing from that bridge, or anywhere I could get hit by a car like that. I told her that the bridges I usually fish were not as bad as that one, which I guess helped some, because she just wound up asking me to be careful out there, even though I could tell she'd be having nightmares about it. I felt bad because my fishing had never worried Cindy in the least before then… but her seeing that bridge had really rattled her cage.

Billy: That's completely understandable, it's dangerous up there. I mean, we've seen some crazy sh!t up there!

71

Rich: You bet! Especially when the OBI [Oak Beach Inn] was still open. The drunks would pour out of there late at night and wind up coming down Ocean Parkway to either the Wantagh or Meadowbrook Parkway. I used to hate when I was on the 3rd and guys would cross over the white line and come up behind you and blare their horn. It would damn near give me a heart attack. Or they'd throw beer bottles at you from cars doing fifty miles per hour. Man, you could really hurt somebody if you hit them in the head!

Billy: You bet! How many times have we seen cars flying down the parkways on the wrong side of the road in the middle of the night, drunks weaving all over, hitting the center dividers and railings… I was on the 3rd one night and this guy comes flying over the bridge, doing like ninety, the wrong way. I watch him go by and I see another car coming the other way, approaching the bridge and I'm thinking, geez, is there going to be a head-on. So I see the other car, it looks like it pulls off to the side, and the guy going the wrong blows past him. Turns out the other car was a State Trooper. He hits the lights, U-turns and runs this guy down before he gets to the 2nd.

Rich: I used to think that those guys running high speed the wrong way was some sort of punk test… you'd see it so often.

Billy: Maybe they were just plain stupid [*laughs*] There was so much stupid stuff going on up on those bridges at night. I had a time once where I jumped up on the rail on the bridge.

Rich: What now?

Billy: I jumped up on the rail… Listen, I'm on the Meadowbrook one night, this guy's coming with speed, and he's drunk, and there's no one on the bridge but him. And I'm almost… do you remember where that little guard post was?

Rich: Yeah… yeah, absolutely.

Billy: Well I'm just past that, between that and the middle, and this guy he's flying. He comes up on the sidewalk, runs across and hits the center divider, bounces off and comes back across toward the sidewalk, like an S-pattern. And I'm thinking, if he does this again, he's going to hit pretty close to where I am. I jumped up on the railing and I'm not jumping yet, but if this guy's going to hit me, then I'm jumping, and the Meadowbrook is the last bridge you'd ever want to jump from. So he hits the center divider again and winds up hitting the railing about ten feet past where I was… Man, my heart was in my throat!

Rich: Whoa!

Billy: And then I was on the 2nd for that big accident, you remember that one?

73

Rich: I do… A guy died if I remember correctly.

Billy: Yeah, really sad. I was on the 2nd Wantagh with another guy, it was the day before Halloween. I'm walking from the south side, on the west side of the bridge, to the north side. I'm almost exactly to the draw and here comes this little Dodge Caravan type vehicle. He's in the middle lane, just coming onto the bridge, so he's down near the base of the bridge, and this black BMW doing like a hundred and change, come up on him so fast. He clips the guy, like that pit maneuver, it wasn't on purpose, he's just drunk.

The little Caravan goes way up in the air, and comes down hard, the BMW goes skidding into the sidewalk, hits the rail, goes up in the air, goes over my head, upside down in slow motion, I'm looking at the complete exhaust and everything under the car, as it went over my head I'm like HOLY SH!T! It lands on its roof on the sidewalk railings and starts sliding down the bridge. I thought for sure that car was going over the bridge, but it slammed into the street light pole, and instead of that knocking it into the water, it snapped it off the railings and back onto the street, and it rolls all the way to the base of the bridge.

I'm like, OH SH!T! I run over to the car. The roof is flat level with the seats and the car is still running, and I'm like HOLY SH!T, I thought everybody in that car was dead. I run over to the other car, and the poor bastard in the little Caravan, listen… he got shot out the back window of the Caravan, and he was dying right there…

74

and his seat belt was still connected. The impact broke the back of his seat and ejected him like a rocket out the back of the car.

So anyway, we call the cops, the whole thing, and the reason I mention this is, they call me up and I had to go down to Valley Stream, where the State Police are. And I'll never forget this, this Sergeant, who I'll call Sarge F, says, "Bill, do you mind, we have to ask you some questions." I was like, "Okay." I had given them my name because I saw the whole accident, and the poor guy in the Caravan died... all he was doing was coming home from work, taking Ocean Parkway, the scenic view, and this asshole, who was blown out of his shorts drunk, crashed into him and killed him. And the idiot, and I thought everybody in the BMW was dead, but he lived, he was just squished down under the dashboard when they cut him out.

Anyway, Sarge F asks me, "What were you doing on the bridge?" I said, "I was fishing." He's like, "What do you mean?" I said, "I fish off the bridges." So, he didn't understand that, because I was a witness and at two o'clock in the morning, they usually don't have witnesses to accidents like this. When they go to court, guys like this guy usually have a million excuses as to why it happened other than it being their fault, you know. So, we went over the accident in detail, and he asks me, "How fast do you think that guy was going?" I said, "I don't know, about a hundred ten, a hundred twenty." He said, "Why would you say that?" I said, "Assuming the guy in

75

the Caravan was doing the speed limit, or a little faster, like most of us would be doing, the BMW came up on him so fast, he had to be doing double the speed limit at least." Turns out when they did the investigation, the guy was doing a hundred and ten.

He interviewed me for about an hour or so. So, I go home and about two weeks later he calls me back in and he goes over the story again... and I asked, "Why are you doing this?" He goes, "Well… your story is very exact." And I said, "Yeah, it should be, I saw the whole f'ing thing." And he goes, "Well, it doesn't normally work that way…" I said, "You know why it works that way?" He says, "No why?" I said, "It's because I don't drink, I don't do drugs, and I got a great memory…" He goes, "Really?" I said, Really…" He goes, "Do you want to be a witness?" I said, "You bet I do!" So, when the case came to court, they plea bargained it out, because their lawyer knew I was a good witness and they didn't want their guy in jail for the next thirty years.

❦ ❦ ❦

Rich: So, I didn't start fishing the bridges until after the moratorium, like in the late, late 80s, and while you were making a name for yourself by racking up impressive numbers of fifties off the bridges… my early years were somewhat less notable. [*laughing*]

Billy: [*laughs*]

Rich: But… but, I did some interesting sh!t back then. Since I was a kid, I've always been drawn to outlaw fishing, I mean, it's one of the things that attracted me to bridge fishing! I just loved those NO PARKING, NO FISHING FROM THE BRIDGE signs. [*laughs*] I wrote a short story that was published about sneaking into the Water Company lake in CT, where I grew up, to catch big pike, and when I moved to Long Island, as an early teen I used to sneak into the private trout streams behind Blydenburg County Park and catch monstrous rainbow trout, I mean these things were giants. So, I've always had that bend in me, you know, and it's still there, even here, down in Virginia, I manage to get myself in trouble. [*laughs*]

Billy: [*laughing*] Oh, what happened now?

Rich: Eh, nothing much. I was fishing down at the base of a bridge and a game warden chased me off. Apparently I missed the sign [*laughs*]. Then I was fishing from the rocks along Rudee Inlet. I guess I missed the sign there too, because the cops chased me off and gave me a stern warning. It was quite a show for the tourists. [*laughs*] I sold my Korkers after that because you can't fish any rocks down here, I guess because it's a tourist area.

Billy: Kind of makes sense, they probably don't want a bunch of kids getting hurt, and law suits. Besides, you're too old for that sh!t anyway.

Rich: Hey, look who's talking… Anyway, back in the late 70s I lived on the north shore, and that's where I used to fish. After rehabbing from my life as a rock star, I went to work at my father's furniture store in Huntington Village, and I did a lot of the furniture deliveries, which meant I got to know the whole area from Cold Spring Harbor to Northport Harbor pretty well. There are miles and miles of shore line, an incredible amount of wealth, and back then, a whole lot of roads with no names, including a few that lead to beach access that I never would have known about, had I not been delivering furniture to those rich people in their mansions.

One of those roads ended in a small paved parking area for several cars, I guess it was local beach access to Long Island Sound. It wasn't gated or anything, so I would go there at night and fish. It was dead quiet and dark, like really dark, as there were no street lights. There were a couple small rock groins near the parking area and to the east. Not far west was the Marshall field estate, what is now Caumsett State Historic Park Preserve, but back then it was still private property, but I figured, in that darkness who's going to know.

I didn't have the Internet back then, or any of its great features, like satellite mode, or 3D, all I had was a beat up old Rand McNally Atlas, and the map of that area showed a fairly prominent point on the Marshall field shore line, not far from where I parked, so of course, I had to know what was down there. Turned out to be a point with another rock groin and a boulder field. I fished that stretch of beach for several falls, and did quite well there.

Billy: What did you fish with? Did you throw bucktails?

Rich: No, no bucktails. The water was fairly shallow and kelpy in places, and lots of rocks. I threw the typical plugs back then, you know, Redfins, Gibbs bottles, Atom 40s, Long-A's, that was pretty much it. I tell you what... wading around in that water in that dark used to creep me out. The footing could get pretty sketchy at times, there were a lot of rocks, but you had to wade out some to get the distance you needed. I got pretty used to the place after a while, but one night I was fishing out by that point, ball deep in the water, and I was adjusting my stance, and something hit the bone of my right foot so hard I thought I had been shot.

I pulled my foot up, turned around, almost fell, and stumbled back to shore, dragging my line behind me. I was totally freaked. I sat down, put my light on and looked at where the pain was, expecting to see a hole in my boot... but there wasn't any! My bone hurt so bad I thought it was broken, I mean I was freaked, I had no idea what had just happened. I reeled my line in, limped back to my car, took off my waders, pulled off my sock and looked at my foot as best I could. I wasn't bleeding, but it was very painful to the touch.

Billy: I think I know what happened.

Rich: Well, I didn't know about them at the time, but if you guessed Mantis Shrimp, you get the rubber cigar. [*laughs*]

Billy: Yup, Mantis Shrimp… nasty things, I don't know how striped bass manage to eat them.

Rich: Me neither. You know, that area around my bone was bruised purple for like two weeks, and I don't bruise ever, and swollen. I had to cut the side out of a sneaker, just to get around.

Billy: You're lucky your bone wasn't broken, those things pack quite a punch.

Rich: It might have been fractured, I don't know, I never went to the doctor… Anyway, there was another sneaky thing I did that worked out really well. I don't know how well you know Cold Spring Harbor, but basically Route 25A runs right along the backside of the harbor, on the east side. There's a fishing pier there, and the town drops a lot of mooring mushrooms that people rent to moor their boats. There's a lot of them. And just north of the fishing pier, the town has a small pier that they tie up a bunch of row boats to, for people to ferry themselves out to their moored boats. And just opposite that pier is this skinny neck of land that comes way out, all the way from the Laurel Hollow side of the bay, to the west, and creates this narrow channel right by the town pier.

So you have Cold Spring Harbor coming in from Long Island Sound and gradually narrowing until it runs into that neck of land and narrow channel. The channel opens into a giant pond that goes back to the fish hatchery and Cold Spring Harbor Laboratories, and back in the late 70s, that whole area would fill up with bunker so thick you could walk on them. I mean massive amounts, in the pond, in the channel, along the neck of land, the whole back bay would load up with bunker.

Billy: Same thing on the south shore. There were lots of bunker everywhere back then, right into the 80s. Remind me to tell you something later, about the bunker.

Rich: If I remember [*laughs*]

Billy: Don't worry, I'll remember.

Rich: Good… So anyway, the public fishing pier ran parallel to shore, and everyone would be lined up snagging bunker, hooking up with big bluefish, tangling up in everybody else's line, it was a clown show. The short version is one night I wandered up to the town pier and noticed that it wasn't gated or monitored, I went out and fished from it. Then I noticed that the rowboats were not locked, they were just tied up to cleats on the dock, with oars in them. I couldn't believe it. I guess the town figured, who'd steal an old wooden row boat, right? [*laughs*]

So I didn't think they'd mind if I borrowed one for a little bit. I can't believe nobody else figured this out. I'd walk out, put my gear in a row boat, and row over to the neck on the opposite side of the channel, beach the rowboat, and fish from shoreline there. I had it all to myself. Turns out that's where the bass were. They'd show up at some point every night, running up and down that neck of land, blowing bunker right up on the beach. That was my first real experience with chunking. I was pretty naïve back then, just fishing by instinct, learning as I go, but that was a pretty cool time. I caught a lot of fish, but nothing that cracked maybe twenty… I don't know, it was a long time ago. I never did get caught taking the row boats though [*laughs*].

Billy: [*laughs*] I guess you couldn't do this during the day.

Rich: No, it was strictly night maneuvers. There was other stuff I did, but back then, what I was best known for was jigging bluefish and weakfish from a particular group of party boats that ran out of Huntington Harbor. Man, we had some good weakfish fishing back then. I actually became good friends with one of the captains and fished on his private boat sometimes. I had a couple friends with boats. I remember one time, I was out on this guy's boat, and we're fishing down by the mouth of the Nissequogue River. He had this Sitex white line recorder, you remember those?

Billy: Of course I do, I owned one. [*laughs*]

Rich: [*laughs*] Anyway, we pull up on this ledge in about thirty feet of water, and his recorder goes black from the bottom up to about four feet off the bottom. We drop our jigs down, oh… back then I didn't use AVA jigs, I used a very slightly tear drop shaped jig with like opposing forty-five degree downward grooves molded into them from the center spine on each side. It's hard to explain. They were finished in a dull chrome, not the usual shiny chrome, and you could fish them with a lot more control than the AVA jigs. And these things were deadly on bass and weakfish. They were only made for a little while locally, and were stamped with the letters TF, and the only place I could get them was the old Four Winds B&T in Huntington. They were called Tiger-Stripe jigs. I bought a lot of them and still have a few left.

So, down go the jigs, we hit bottom, a couple slow cranks and bang, we're in. We get the fish up and they're weakfish, nice weakfish, like eight, nine pound fish. Back down, same thing. We had a perfect drift along that ledge and had those fish under the boat for like half a mile. Largest weak was probably was around eleven or twelve pounds. That was probably the best weakfish fishing I ever had for quality weakfish.

Billy: Nice! But you want to talk about weakfish, listen to this… Remember before, when I said, "Remind me to tell you something later". Well, what I wanted to tell you had to do with bunker and weakfish. Through the 70s and into the early 80s I continued to catch big bass, and I had caught a lot of them, some years more than others, but there were always big fish around. But somewhere around 83, I began to notice that there weren't as many fish around. I was fishing just as hard, but I wasn't finding as many fish, it was definitely noticeable.

But here's where you can make a case for when one species declines, other species fill the void. It was 84, 85, and 86, I'll remember that for the rest of my life. So in early October of 84, I go up there, this is the Meadowbrook I'm talking about, the bridge was loaded with bunker, acres of bunker, I mean they were on both sides, north and south, out two hundred yards. There were so many bunker that if you threw a cast net you wouldn't be able to move it, you know what I mean… acres of them, and they were big bunker.

You know when bunker separate, and they make a big circle in the middle with nothing in it, so you know that there's a fish there. Well, I was like, what the hell is that, because I knew it wasn't a bass, I just didn't know what it was. I didn't even think about big weakfish, I hadn't seen a big weakfish in twenty years. So, I snagged a bunker and dropped it down, and I get a run-off immediately, right. This things running, and I set the hook… nothing. I'm like, nothing? So I do it again, same thing… nothing!

So I'm thinking, it definitely ain't bass, you just can't miss bass, especially the way I hook bunker, and I'm trying to think of a fish that would do that, and weakfish aren't even in my mind, you know. So I treble hook a bunker, right through his nose, and let this thing run, like run,

run, and finally set the hook. I got him! And he's a good fish, but it's not a bass, you know, and I come up with this huge weakfish, it was like sixteen pounds. I was stunned… and then we started to catch big weakfish.

Now the night Dennis Rooney caught the world record nineteen pound two ounce, I weighed in an eighteen nine at Skippy's in East Rockaway and me and another guy had a dozen fish over seventeen pounds, you know. I think the world record at the time, I don't know, I could be wrong, but I think the world record at that time was around sixteen nine, whatever… even if it was little bit bigger, we had a half a dozen fish as big, or bigger than the current world record. And then Dennis Rooney got it with the nineteen two and—

Rich: He got that in the State Channel right?

Billy: Huh?

Rich: He got that fish in the State Channel didn't he.

Billy: No! He got that out front of The Meadowbrook Bridge, in front of the, um… right by the bay houses there.

Rich: Oh OK, OK, I know where that is.

Billy: Yeah, that whole area was loaded with bunker and gigantic weakfish… Listen, I'll never forget this. I took a friend out, he'd never caught a weakfish in his life, ever. I called him up and said do you want to catch the biggest weakfish of your life, he said yeah. I said can you come up at two in the morning, because we had a really late tide, and those fish were only on the outgoing tide, you know.

So he meets me up there. I had a rod set up for him, I snag a bunker and put it on his rod, right away he hooks up. The fish weighed sixteen pounds. And get this, there were zero bass on the bridge while those weakfish were there, for a couple of years, not one, no bass, it was all big, giant weakfish, from September into October. It wasn't until those weakfish left in October each year, that a few big bass would start showing up into November. There weren't a lot of them, I mean, I'd go four or five nights without seeing a fish and then one night maybe I'd see two. It was tough fishing for bass back then.

Rich: Wow... I'm sorry I missed those weakfish! I mean, we had some good years on the north shore for weakfish right around that same time, you know, but by then, I had been living on the south shore for several years and was fishing both shores. I don't think those big fish made it down to Great South Bay or I would have heard about it. There were always weakfish in the GSB, but not like those... then again, I could be wrong.

Billy: Well, catching those big weakfish was fun, but nothing could get my heart beating faster than seeing a big bass in the shadow line. That was always the thing about bridge fishing, like one thing that always amazed me was, I had times where I would say… say I parked my truck on the southwest side of the Meadowbrook, during the incoming, and I'd walk completely across the bridge to the north side, and I'd walk back. And when I left there were no fish on the south side, and by the time I'd walk back to the north side, there'd be one or two big fish under one of the lights.

I'd be like, holy crap, they just came out of nowhere. And then there were times you'd be fishing, and a big fish would come right up in front of you, you know, and you'd get that rush. Stuff like that, that's what made bridge fish so exciting… you just never knew… Even now, some fifty years later, there is nothing that could make my heart beat faster than seeing a big fish pop up in the shadow line. Unfortunately, those fish aren't around anymore.

Hey, listen to this. You tell me if this is bad luck, or bad decision making. I'm on the bridge one night, and it's the first time in my life I ignored the little voice in my head telling me that I should do something. I'm one of those guys that when I believe I should do something, I don't hesitate, I just do it, I never second guess myself, you know. So I have a good fish on, not tremendous, about a forty-four, forty-five pound fish, something like that, and I'm walking him down, and my friend comes over the bridge in his pickup truck, sees me, pulls up and says, "Greek, what do you got." I said, "I got a good fish." So he says, "I'll pull over and run down and get him for you."

As I'm walking the fish down to him, I see this enormous bass sitting with his nose against the shadow line… I mean this fish is way bigger than the one I have on. And I stop dead in my tracks. The tide has got my fish pushed back up against the bridge, about five feet or so behind where this other bass is, up in the shadow line, and I remember thinking to myself that I should just cut my line and go for this other fish, he was so big. The fish I had on would be fine, he'd shake the bucktail in a heartbeat, I'd tie on another bucktail and try for that big fish in the shadow line, right.

Instead, I walked my fish behind him really slow, and the fish didn't move, so once I got down a little bit further, I literally horsed my fish down to the shore line. My friend gets the fish out, unhooks it, and he's yelling, "I got it!" I didn't even care what he was saying, I was already running back to where that big fish was, and it was gone!

Rich: [*laughing loudly*]

Billy: And I never forgave myself, I said you stupid [*expletive*]. I had the opportunity to cut this BS forty pound fish off and go for that really big fish, like I knew I should have, but instead I fooled myself, because when I went by him a span or so, I looked back and he was still there, so I figured alright, he's not going nowhere. And when I came back up, he was gone! I was so pissed, I couldn't talk! [*laughs*]

Rich: [*laughing*]

Billy: So was that bad luck, or just a bad choice?

Rich: Hard to say… I mean, when you cut your line, the wind could have blown it on to bass's back, and the bass would have bolted… or while you were tying on a new bucktail, the fish could have just dropped out of the shadow line, you just don't know. Then you wouldn't have even had the forty.

Billy: Nah, I don't buy the line thing, but I guess you never know… but man, I really wanted to catch that big fish. I was so freak'in mad.

Rich: Yeah, I bet they heard you all the way over at the Fundy.

Billy: [*laughs*]

So, the moratorium arrived in 85. All of the attendant symptoms were there, small fish, and some really big fish, but missing were quantities of the middle classes of twenties, thirties and forties. Billy still managed to catch at least one fifty during the moratorium and each of the subsequent years during the rebuilding period. I began fishing the bridges in the very late 80s and had been fishing both shores for a number of years by that time, and through our collaboration on this book, we've seemed to have uncovered a bit of a mystery.

While talking about the late 80s and years 90 and 91, when the keeper size limit was thirty-six inches, I had mentioned that in 89 and 90, catching keepers was fairly common. Just as a reference, a thirty-six inch striped bass is twelve years old and weighs around twenty pounds or so. That's not a fish that came to be as a result of the moratorium. And then Billy was talking about how in 91, he had a bunch of fifties, and a lot of forties on the Meadowbrook. We also noted that twenty-five pound fish were a dime a dozen, and there were a fair amount of thirties in the mix also. And from 92 to 98, striped bass of all sizes were all over the bridges.

So, where did these fish come from? All of those weight classes are way too old to have come from any effect of the moratorium. And we're not talking a few fish here, and a few fish there, were talking a massive amount of those middle and upper weight classes of fish that were missing during the moratorium. Billy has video from around 97 of himself fishing on his boat, where he's averaging thirty to forty fish a tide, and every day he'd have eight or ten fish over forty pounds. Even back then, Billy was asking himself where those fish came from.

So, when we got to the stage of this book where we were having conversations about the post-moratorium period, we got into some intense discussions about this apparent anomaly in the striped bass stocks. Billy knew that I had done an exhaustive independent assessment of the bass stocks back in 2017, and that I had examined the period of the moratorium recovery extensively, as part of the assessment. He asked me if my data could offer any insight as to the presence of all those fish. I told him no, that as far as I could tell, most of those year classes shouldn't even have existed, at least not in the numbers we were seeing at the time. My assessment clearly shows that while a great sequence of Hudson YOY (Young Of The Year) year classes, coupled with some massive Chesapeake YOY year classes, would create a great fishery starting in the late 90s, it could not account for those fish.

So, where did they come from? My only guess would be they were from the Hudson River stock, and it can only be a guess because there was no YOY data kept for the Hudson River prior to 1985. And even if those fish were Hudson stock, that still doesn't answer the question of where they were in those several years surrounding the moratorium in 85. Maybe they just bypassed the South Shore and migrated to and from the Hudson by way of Long Island Sound for a couple years. It's possible, they're fish, they have fins, they can swim where ever they want to. But somehow, this explanation doesn't seem to hold water, so for Billy and I, this will always remain a mystery, or as that paint instructor on PBS, Bob Ross, used to say, "A happy accident."

Billy with the fifty-nine pound bass you'll read about later. He liked to put plugs in their mouths so that people thought he caught them on the beach instead of the bridges.

The Great Recovery…

If you were a striped bass fisherman on Long Island back around 1990, then for the next couple of decades or so, you got to partake in an embarrassment of bass fishing riches that this current generation of bass fishermen (2025) will never experience, and future generations will only be able to dream about. Some of us lived through it, and most striped bass fishermen are aware of the fact, that there was once a moratorium on striped bass fishing, back in 1985. Based on the current state of the stocks, due to what I attribute to poor resource management, this may actually happen again. But back in 85 conditions were different, and a quick look back will show why those of us who fished the waters of the New York area were the most fortunate, in terms of striped bass biomass recovery.

While I'll never be able to account for the appearance of all those middle and upper class size fish we had in the late 80s and early 90s, I will point out that there were not a lot of smaller size fish around during that same time. Those fish didn't start showing up en masse until about the late 90s, right about the time the YOY data indicated they would, and it's the only thing that seemed to make sense about the data for that time period. The rest of the data paints a clear picture of the epic striped bass recovery that took place, from around the mid-90s, right on through the next two decades.

Here's a quick overview. The total Atlantic Striped Bass Biomass (SSB) is made up of seventy-five percent Chesapeake Bay fish, and twenty-five percent Hudson fish, and it's the Hudson fish that saved our bacon during the lean years following the moratorium in 1985. While the Chesapeake YOY continued to drop steadily from 1971 on through the moratorium in 1985, until its first excellent YOY class in 1989, the Hudson River experienced record YOY classes for four consecutive years spanning 1987 to 1990. The Hudson then continued to produce excellent YOY classes almost every other year, right up until 2003. And while the Hudson stock only contributes roughly twenty-five percent to the total SSB, the consistently excellent YOY classes added up quickly. The fact that Hudson fish basically do not migrate south, made those of us who plied the waters of New York, and north of us, the beneficiaries.

Conversely, the Chesapeake stock, which again, makes up seventy-five percent of the total SSB, finally got its first successful YOY class in 1989, four years after the moratorium was lifted in New York, and it was a big one. The striped bass recovery got its second kick in 1993 when Maryland recorded the highest YOY class index since they had been keeping records. That record was completely shattered in 1996 with the best YOY class

94

index ever recorded. They had to remake the chart to fit this one in! Then in 2001, the second highest YOY index was recorded.

Those freakishly massive spawns in the Chesapeake, coupled with the consistently above average spawns in the Hudson created a perfect storm of year class recruitments that would flood our local waters with striped bass for several decades. It would be the best striped bass fishing anyone in our generation would ever experience, EVER. It would also provide the framework from which the ASMFC would extract the data it used as the basis for its folly of a management plan, a plan, that in my opinion, completely failed to proactively protect the striped bass and avoid the stock crash we are experiencing today.

At the time of this writing in 2025, people are still catching striped bass. There are fish around, no doubt about that, and it may be easy to think that there is no problem with the fishery. But those fish are the remnants of the last two large Chesapeake YOY year classes of 2011 and 2015, plus whatever the Hudson River stock has been chipping in. Problem is, there has been little to no recruitment from either the Chesapeake or the Hudson stocks for several years now, so when those fish are gone, what's left to replace them? If you pay attention to such things, you'll notice that the fish that are still around are not widespread. They'll show up here and there, but other areas will be dead. Anglers must wait and hope those fish pay them a visit at some point. Spring and fall migrations are quick, the bites are short-lived in most places, and very few places on the striper coast will hold resident fish. And it's not going to get better any time soon.

Conversely, during the peak of the striped bass recovery, there were so many fish, at times, they seemed to be everywhere, all at once. It was fish on demand. Each spring, the striped bass would roar up the coast, pour out of the Hudson, and flood the whole Striper Coast with fish. The fall migration would start somewhere around the end of August and last right into December, with solid fishing the entire time. There's a video on YouTube taken by a well-known surf fisherman and author, of one of the massive white bait blitzes at Montauk that were typical in the fall during this time. You can hear his voice on the video describing it as "fish porn". There were so many fish, they were even around in the summer months, if you knew where to look.

Fishing was so good that sport fishing publications couldn't fit every fishing report given to them on its pages, Bait &Tackle shops were busy weighing fish and selling bait, and pictures of big bass were tacked all over the walls and on display at all the counters. Yep, business was booming. What this period of time meant to those of us who fished the west end bridges was that those fish would storm into the West End bays every spring and fall, and take up residence around the nine west end bridges. The key word here is "residence", a concept that most striped bass fishermen of the time failed to grasp, or more specifically, the concept of "resident fish", those fish that set up on the bridge structure and never left..

The bay is home to every kind of bait fish that inhabits our local waters. This includes all the usual suspects like menhaden aka bunker, both adult and peanut, white bait, such as spearing, bay anchovies and the like, and a variety of species generally not associated as bait items for striped bass, but are all on the menu, such as, porgies, blackfish, lizardfish, seabass, and other ground fish. These are all naturally drawn to the bridges, either because of the structure the bridges provided, or by being attracted to the light cast by the street lights at night. To a bass, this is an all you can eat buffet, open twenty-four hours a day, seven days a week. The variety of bait fish I would see inside the stomachs of the fish I would occasionally keep for the table was astounding.

I don't think striped bass fishermen on Long Island appreciated what they had back then. More specifically, I don't think they realized how unique Long Island's South Shore Bay system truly is, and how lucky they were, and are, to have it. Back then, it was a completely under-utilized resource. In the spring and fall there would be so many resident fish in so many places that you could almost walk on their backs, and while there was a fair amount of boat activity in the inlets, and some around the Robert Moses Bridge, there was very little effort made by shore bound anglers to unlock the bays true potential, and man, did they miss out!

Thus far, I've made a lot of bridge fishing references that most people probably don't fully understand. To get the full benefit of our stories, here's a quick primer on the basic practices of fishing from a bridge. Obviously, you are either fishing the incoming tide or the outgoing tide, and the side of the bridge you fish determines whether you are fishing "into the tide" or "under the bridge" otherwise known as the "downtide" side of the bridge. When you fish into the tide, the current is moving toward you. You can fish into the tide a couple of different ways. First you can target fish you can see on the surface, in the shadow lines cast by the streetlights.

The other technique is to blind cast beyond the shadow line, and work the bucktail on the bottom, as the current pushes the jig toward you, into the shadow line targeting fish you cannot see that are lying on the bottom. In either case, these fish will stem the tide, head facing into the current, in the dark shadow area, with their noses right up against the shadow line, just before the artificially lit portion of the water. This is their ambush point, the bait fish are drawn to the light, the bass hide in the dark, pretty basic stuff.

Another way of thinking about it would be standing in a dark house looking out into a well-lit parking lot. You (the bass) can easily see out of the house, but someone outside in the parking lot (the baitfish) could not easily see you inside the house. This scenario produces the feeding advantage that draws the predator striped bass into the dark of the shadow line to prey on hapless baitfish attracted to the artificial streetlights of the bridge. The disadvantage to fishing into the tide is that hooked fish use the current to run under the bridge, which can make it difficult to land them.

When you fish under the bridge, aka the downtide side of the bridge, the current is coming out from underneath the bridge and moving away from you. This is primarily structure fishing, and in order to fish the structure, you are employing the looping swing cast that I described earlier, during my initial introduction to the 3rd Wantagh Bridge. You cast the bucktail out from the bridge and swing it back up underneath and work the bottom structure in the direction the tide is moving. This technique requires a good deal of practice to do effectively, and is used exclusively on the west side of the 2nd and 3rd Wantagh bridges during the outgoing tide, due to the high chain link fences that are in place on the east sides of the bridges.

We did fish into the outgoing tide on the east side from fence stands for a while, but that came with a host of problems, and we gave up on it after a while. The looping swing cast can also be used on other bridges, but was basically developed, out of necessity, for fishing the Wantagh bridges. The advantage of fishing under the bridge is that hooked fish tend to run with the current out away from the bridge, but not always. Hopefully this little treatise will help you visualize some of what you've heard so far, and will hear, about how we fished from atop the bridges.

One of the many striped bass over fifty pounds Billy has caught in the decades he has fished the west end bridges.

Different Strokes & Orbits

There were not a lot of people fishing the bridges when I first started back in the very late 80s. It was post moratorium, and those who were there before me had endured tough fishing during that time, and they were not particularly excited to see any new faces showing up on the bridges. It was a territorial thing. I knew this going in, so I wasn't expecting any kumbaya welcomes, and I can testify that I certainly didn't receive any. So, I kept to myself as I learned my craft, and other than one quick dust up on the 2nd Wantagh Bridge, within a couple years I eventually became part of the every-night landscape of those who fished the west end bridges.

That first year I didn't see Billy very much, and when I did, he was just passing through, looking for big fish. I was busy figuring out how it all worked, as different bridges were fished different ways, and had different obstacles to overcome, or techniques to learn. But one thing became clear to me right away. I was not going to try and turn myself into a Billy clone. I wasn't going to try and follow in his footsteps, or try and emulate his successes. The truth is, Billy is Billy, there is only one of him, and he is unique. But it actually went a little deeper than that.

First, there are his physical attributes. For starters, his balance is off the charts. He reminds me of those native American iron workers who would walk on the I-beams forty stories up, building skyscrapers. He has absolutely no fear of heights. He walked the little ledges on the outside of the Meadowbrook and Loop Parkway bridges, like it was a walk in the park. And he's got the vision of an eagle, better than twenty-twenty. He can see fish in the shadow line of a bridge that nobody else can see, and see them from a long way off.

Despite the fact that I was a gymnast in high school, I was never going to be comfortable fishing the ledge side of the Big M and Loop Parkway Bridge without the safety harness I rigged up for myself. But it proved to be cumbersome while walking fish down, and after struggling with it for a while, I simply gave up fishing those two areas. But it didn't really matter, because right around the time I chucked my harness, those ledges were done away with when they resurfaced the bridges.

But the other physical attribute I was never going to have was Billy's ability to spot fish in the shadow line. I wore glasses, so the ambient street light reflecting off the lenses caused problems for me, and the slight astigmatism in my left eye didn't help much either. It would be many years before I finally figured out a method of spotting bass in the shadow line, but I still wasn't great at it.

Several years after I had been fishing the bridges, when I had pretty much made the Wantagh bridges my home base, Billy stopped down at the 2nd Wantagh Bridge one night while I was fishing. I was the only one on the bridge that night. The tide was outgoing and I was on the southwest side, casting back up under the bridge. I had been picking away at fish through the tide, but took a break when Billy showed up. We talked for a few minutes. He hadn't found any monsters on any of the other bridges yet, so he said, "Let's go over to the other side and see if there's anything in the shadow line."

I said, "Okay."

We hopped the railing and ran across the parkway, over to the entrance of the bike path on the other side. We walked out to the second light and Billy shot up the eight foot chain link fence and then swung his leg over the top and sat up, kind of leg-locked, on top of the wobbly fence. He looked down at me and said, "What are you waiting for?"

I climbed up the fence, but when I got to the top I planted my toes into the chain link, and hung my arms over the side, and leaned there supported by my armpits.

He said, "What are you doing, get up here!"

I said, "No way man, ain't happening. I can see just fine from here."

He started laughing, "What are you chicken!"

"Solid yellow, go ahead laugh all you want, I'm not getting up there… you're f'ing nuts."

So after he's done busting my balls, Billy looks down into the shadow line and immediately he points between the ice breakers.

"Look at that! There's three nice fish right there, see'em!"

103

I look to where he's pointing and try as I might, I can't see the fish. I see the lit water and I see the dark water where the fish are, but I can't see past the sheen on the surface of the dark water to see the fish.

"No…nope, I can't see them."

He couldn't believe it. "You can't see those fish! Are you kidding me!"

"No Billy, I can't see those fish, what do you want me to tell you!"

Shaking his head, Billy said, "Man, you got to be f'ing blind. They're like three logs laying in the water, I don't know how you could miss them… You know, I could catch those fish."

At that point my frustration got the better of me. "Yeah, I bet you could. After all, you are the greatest fisherman that ever lived!"

Instead of being pissed, he just burst out laughing as he casually swung his leg over the top of the fence and quickly climbed down to the bike path. He could be really blunt at times in his younger days, but he's always had a great sense of humor.

"C'mon," he said laughing, "let's go back over and catch a few more fish before the tide dies."

So aside from the fact that I did not possess the x-ray eyes and fearlessness that Billy possessed, there was one other basic difference between us. Billy's goal has always been to catch big fish, fifty pound and over fish, a world record striped bass, that's been his go juice since the beginning and it's what he's known for. But that's not how I'm wired. While Billy's objective has always been size, my objective has always been numbers, or more accurately knowing, as in knowing how to rack up big numbers. There's actually much more to it than that, but that's another story, for another time. Now, I'm not saying that I didn't seek out big fish, because through the years I caught plenty, but at the end of the night, it was always about numbers for me, and wanting to know more. And to put up big numbers every night, you had to go to the source and unlock the secrets, and it was for that reason I made the Wantagh bridges my home.

The problem was the Wantagh bridges were, without a doubt, the most difficult bridges to fish. None of the other six bridges came anywhere close. The 3rd Wantagh was the worst of the three, but it was also the bridge that consistently held more fish, by far, night after night, than any of the other west end bridges. The reason it was the worst bridge to fish, and also held the most fish, had everything to do with the underwater topography beneath the bridge. To say that it was bizarre is basically an understatement. When you consider that most of the other bridges have smooth sandy bottoms, it's hard to conceive of what could have created the havoc that was the bay bottom beneath the 3rd Wantagh Bridge.

For starters, on the outgoing tide it had the strongest currents of any of the nine bridges by far. You had water coming from the south from Stone Creek, water coming from the north as Zach's Bay drained out, and finally a huge push of water coming from the east, from South

Oyster Bay, bouncing off the Black Banks, all converging at the bridge. The outgoing currents were immensely strong, especially on an east wind, and during the moon periods they were absolutely savage. To make it more interesting, all that water was running over the most bizarre bottom structure you can imagine.

The deepest point of the bridge was around thirty-two feet, but every span was an adventure in itself, and the depths varied greatly from span to span, and even within some spans! There were humps, bumps, ridges, holes, you name it, and every one of them was a snag waiting to happen. The only explanation I can think of for those unusually pronounced bottom contours, was that during an earlier rebuilding of the bridge, they must have dumped much of the concrete straight down into the water, in effect, creating an artificial reef beneath the bridge.

How else could you explain a ridge coming up to within ten feet of the surface, way back under the bridge, dropping down toward you to about seventeen feet, and then another ridge coming up abruptly right beneath your feet, before dropping off to about twenty feet just off the bridge. And all of this covered in barnacles, muscles, lost anchor ropes, and anything else that happened to find its way in there.

But that bottom structure was the key to what made the 3rd Wantagh hold the prodigious numbers of striped bass that it did, night after night, after night. In the sandy bottom of the west end bays, that bottom structure, covered in barnacles, muscles, kelp, green crabs, blue crabs, and all manner of invertebrates, was its own

106

miniature ecosystem, providing food to just about every bait fish and ground fish that frequented our local waters. In turn, striped bass came in droves and took up residence, to feed on the easy pickings the bridge offered. There was no reason for them to ever leave. During the peak of the striped bass recovery, that bridge held hundreds and hundreds of fish at a time, probably more, I really have no way of knowing for sure.

A little ways down the road, the 2nd Wantagh Bridge was not quite as challenging as the 3rd, but it too had a fairly steep learning curve before you could expect to reap her full bounty. The 2nd was a drawbridge, so you basically had two sections to fish, the northwest side and the southwest side. The southwest side was the much deeper side and generally deeper than the 3rd Wantagh, but somewhat less snaggy.

None the less, it still had its fair share of boulders, ridges, holes, snags, and like the 3rd Wantagh, every span was unique. All of that you had to learn, and all of that took time. The northwest side was a different story. It had a cable grouping or something that created a ridge line that ran directly below the walkway railing, from near shore all the way out to the bridge operator's tower. The ridge was about eight to ten feet beneath the surface, but dropped straight off on either side to much deeper water.

That entire ridge could hold fish at times, and on both tides. It too, had become over grown with muscles and kelp, and was particularly sticky. And while the water on this side of the bridge could at times be plagued with a leafy green seaweed that floated through on the outgoing tide, that same ridge was very productive on the incoming tide, which, for whatever reason, did not have the same problem with that leafy weed. As a result, I fished this bridge quite often on the incoming tide. In spite of the chain link fence, this was also a bridge where I was able to learn to fish into the outgoing tide from a very specific spot on the southeast shore. It took a long time, the right equipment, and a lot of effort to find the sweet spot and timing, but all I can say is, WOW, it was well worth the effort.

The 1st Wantagh Bridge was kind of an enigma to me initially. I didn't pay a whole lot of attention to it when I first started fishing the bridges, choosing instead to focus most of my time and energy on the 3rd Wantagh, simply because I knew that's where most of the fish would be. Nobody talked about the 1st, at all, and I never saw any activity there as I drove by each night. But I couldn't forget about those little paths I saw on either side of the parkway that disappeared down the slopes, to the shore areas below.

Suffice it to say that the 1st Wantagh Bridge is the deepest bridge in the bay, meaning it is the furthest bridge from Jones inlet, and that all fishing associated with this bridge, is done from the shore areas around it. Eventually, those little paths got the better of me, and over time, the 1st Wantagh did reveal her very special secrets to me.

Going back to the time Billy introduced me to the west end bridges, my free-wheeling days and nights of living by the cue stick were coming to an end. A couple of my friends from my other life, in the technical sector, had a start-up company and wanted to bring me on board. The money wasn't great, but it did have medical benefits, and considering that I had been skating by without any medical coverage, for a prolonged period of time, I figured it was about time to get my life back in order. Besides, the hours were flexible, work when you get in, go home when you're tired. Not a bad transition actually. Besides, I think my brain needed the challenge.

Fortunately for me, I've always had a roaring metabolism and never really required a lot of sleep to function, so the transition went fairly quickly and without much pain. I jumped straight into work, knowing these guys well, and knowing what they wanted from me, and after work, I'd grab a quick nap and head straight out to the 3rd Wantagh Bridge. It was nearing the end of August and I only had less than a month before bass would begin to show up on the bridge, so I had a lot to learn in a short period of time. I didn't have a lot of money at the time, so I stayed with the gear that I had used the night Billy took me out on my tour of the bridges. The only difference was that I brought along a healthy supply of two and three ounce bank sinkers, instead of bucktails. I figured it was better to map out the bottom losing cheap sinkers, than losing two dollar and fifty cent bucktails, and I was right. And so began my crash course of the 3rd Wantagh Bridge.

I parked on the southwest side of the bridge, which I would later learn, is where pretty much everybody who fished that bridge parked, and made the conscious decision to focus my attention on learning that side of the bridge first. I decided on the first three spans and spent all of my time and effort trying to mentally map out the bottom contour of each span, basically by trial and error. To make matters worse, I was still struggling with mastering the art of the under the bridge, loop cast.

The problem is that in order to figure out the bottom contour, and potential snags, you had to be able to make consistent distance casts back under the bridge. Then you could count down until you touch bottom, so you'd know when to lift your rod to keep from getting stuck in a snag. Then you needed to determine whether the bottom dropped, or came up, which told you how much, if any, you had to crank in line. Then you had to figure out if you were going to run into a ridge and where it was, and how many cranks of the handle, and/or fast lift of the rod would clear it, then how much line to let out on the drop back after clearing it. And this was just one pass over one small section of one span. There was a hell of a lot of mechanics involved in fishing this bridge.

So even though bank sinkers don't have hooks to hang into things, I still lost a whole bunch initially, because basically I was flying blind, and there was so much down there to know. It's one of the reasons why that bridge never got too crowded. Guys would come up to give it a try, lose four or five bucktails in half an hour, say f this, leave, and you'd never see them again. But as I started to become more familiar with the different depths, and more adept and consistent with my casting technique, I started moving back and forth through those three spans quicker.

As I mentally mapped out the bottom contours, it never failed to amaze me just how different each span could be from each other, as well as the crazy variations within each one. Every span was a trip, and over time I wound up giving them names, usually associated with the structure or character of the span. The first span became "Double Ridge Big Rock". The second span became "Flat Ridge" and was the span I caught my very first striped bass from a couple months later. The third span got named "The Washing Machine" for the wicked upwelling that existed at the end of a shallow chute that dropped abruptly off into deep water. During a moon tide, that weird foldback of water was so strong it could float a two ounce bucktail.

Aside from the gargantuan task of crash coursing myself on the casting technique and bottom structure mapping of the first three spans of the bridge, I had to deal with the reality that eventually I would have to land a fish. This meant that I had to do some test runs getting over the fence and hopping down the rocks to the water's edge. Fortunately for me, I was a gymnast in high school, and the pommel horse was one of the apparatus that I had performed on, so the one-handed swing your left leg over, swing your right leg over, hop down on the other side of the fence maneuver, was easy as pie for me. One down.

Then came figuring out how to get down the rocks. And just for reference, these rocks make up a slope that is around forty-five degrees and your travel distance on them is probably close to twenty feet to shore. To say those rocks were intimidating is definitely an understatement, as they certainly scared the hell out of me during my initial encounter. Having to go down those rock slopes to land a fish, was another reason why I think the bridges never got too crowded, despite how good the fishing was. Many people were terrified of those rocks. I'd see guys that didn't even have fish on, they just wanted to get to the bottom to fish, slowly crabbing their way down the rocks on their butts, all arms and legs. And I can't blame them, that's the way I went down them for the first time, when trying to figure it all out. I wasn't even sure at that point if I would be able to hop down the rocks while fighting a fish.

So after crabbing my way to the bottom, I did some exploring trying to figure out where a good place to land a fish would be. Amongst the bottom rubble of shoreline rocks, there was this one, large, flat rock, a little ways out from the base of the bridge, that jumped out at me like a sign post that read, ALL FISH GET LANDED HERE! It was that obvious! With a minimal amount of investigation, the landing path down the rocks had revealed itself to me, albeit, in reverse. All I had to do was work it backward, and figure out my way back up to the top from the landing rock.

So, I looked at the rocks, figured which foot I would be leading with, and then which rock was next, and with what foot, and so forth, until the long flat sloped rock about two-thirds of the way up, that you took several steps on before stepping off onto another rock, until I got to the top.

Then I turned and looked back down at the rocks and the path that I had just climbed up. I knew that I needed to be able to go down that same path on my feet, or everything I was doing was for nothing. It was either fold the hand, or go all in, so I took a deep breath and went down, SLOWLY, THOUGHTFULLY, on my feet, for the first time, down to the landing rock. I don't mind telling you that I thought I was going to crap my pants, I mean, it was really scary. My brain kept telling me what could go wrong, in the middle of the night, with no one around. Look, you take a header on those rocks, the best case scenario is broken bones, a lot of broken bones, if you're lucky. But in reality, the chances are, you're cracking your skull wide open, end of story.

So I went back up, and went down again, and a couple more times after that. You know, until I wrote this book, I hadn't thought of those rocks in decades. After three or four hundred times up and down those rocks, I never even gave them a second thought while landing a fish, or any of the other rocks either. It's strange what you can get used to.

After all the cramming I did for my big test, I wound up getting cold feet come late September, the traditional beginning of the season. I guess I just didn't feel ready to go up there and fish yet, particularly if there were going to be others there, or more specifically, regulars there, those who didn't want me around. Because of that insecurity, I didn't go up on the 3rd for my first time, until well into the season, sometime around the third week of

113

October. It was a late night outgoing tide, a nice night, not much wind. As I came over the bridge, I saw two guys fishing the north side, and when I pulled into the parking area, there was only one truck, so I guess they had come together. I had hoped that nobody would be there.

Feeling more than a little nervous, I walked to the beginning of the bridge and stood there for a few minutes, just running everything through my mind before walking out onto the bridge. There was no traffic at that time of night, and being out in the middle of nowhere, you got that weird paradox where it is so quiet, that you can hear everything. I could hear the water rushing up against the bridge pilings, the screech of far off seagulls, even the sound of road sand grinding under my sneakers as I walked, seemed unusually loud. The light breeze was filled with the distinct tang of salt and the scent of baitfish. In fact, all my senses seemed to be much sharper than usual.

I walked out to the first span and looked down into the dark outgoing water rushing out into the bay. My moment had come and it was time to get to it. I unhooked the two ounce Smiling Bill bucktail, with a #70 Uncle Josh pork rind trailer from my rod, and took up a familiar position at the railing. My first loop cast back under the bridge was kind of a chicken, test cast, to make sure everything was operating okay. I let it run through with the current, not expecting it to make any contact with the bottom or rocks, and it didn't. The next cast, I put more into it and went further back. I put the reel in gear and counted down, then lifted the rod and gave the reel a couple cranks. I ticked off the ridge, then a second later bounced off the rock in front of it. I was in the zone.

I moved a few steps to my right, out further onto the bridge, and made another cast. My crash-coursing was paying dividends as I just ticked the ridge at the right time, and I felt that I was getting my rhythm. I moved a few more steps to the right and repeated the process. It was going well. I fished that whole span with only one quick snag, and that I was able to yank free. While the excitement of fishing the bridge was very strong, and my senses were dialed up to eleven, I had yet to feel the one thing I was waiting for.

I moved to the next span. I started near the left piling thinking that maybe a bass would be lurking behind it, looking for an easy meal being washed by in the current. As it turns out, this is not a bad move when fishing the bridges, and in future trips I always made a point to make a pass by the pilings, when working up and down the spans. I learned a few other tricks around the pilings also. Well, the pass by the piling yielded nothing, so I moved to the right a few steps. This span had a very pronounced straight, flat, predictable ridge, right beneath the walkway, so it was an easier span to fish because you could see your line coming up on it, out from under the bridge. Never the less, it was sticky as hell, so if you didn't pay attention, or were too deep, your bucktail would smack straight into it, and you weren't getting it back.

After a few more casts, I wound up somewhere near the middle of the span. I was still in total focus mode. I made a perfect cast back under the bridge, perfect landing, not a bit of bird nest in my spool, just engage the reel and start counting, rod tip pointing down toward the water. I see the line start coming out from under the bridge, I start reeling, about three quick cranks of the reel if I remember correctly, and start slowly raising my rod tip. At this point, I just want to tick over the top of the ridge, the tick letting me know that I didn't blow over the ridge so high as to be out of the strike range.

The pink fifty pound Ande mono line was now clearly visible directly below me, illuminated by the street light on my left, and I felt the bucktail tick the top of the ridge as it washed over in the current. A second later, the unmistakable double tap of a striped bass hitting the bucktail startled me. I was so tightly wound, so uber-focused on casting, counting, lifting, not getting snagged, rinse and repeat, that I was caught off guard and completely missed the hit. The moment I had worked so hard for had come, and I had blown it! I couldn't f'ing believe it! I was so mad that my first impulse was to throw my rod off the bridge.

But I didn't. I cranked my line up, stringing together curse words in combinations I'm not sure they've ever been in before. I should have calmed myself before taking the next cast, but I didn't. The back cast underneath the bridge was sloppy and I over-spooled the reel a little on landing, so I had to quickly thumb the spool, pull out some line to get the excess out, then quickly engage the reel and crank like mad to get the line in, before I snag on the bottom. I managed to accomplish this, but now I was flying blind, as I had to rely on my limited instinct as to where my bucktail was in the water column. Would I slam into the back of the ridge, or would I fly over the top of it, far out of the strike zone? I was talking to myself.

I saw my line coming out from under the bridge and took a quick look down at my reel. I did some quick math in my head on how many yanks of line I pulled out to clear the over-spool and how many cranks of the reel to put it back on, and figured I was close. I put a couple quick cranks on the reel and started to lift the rod tip. As my line came out from beneath the bridge, I didn't feel the tick of the ridge, but like horse shoes and hand grenades, I must have been close enough, because just about the time I was thinking that I missed the mark, Mr. Bass came knocking!

This time I made no mistake and I slammed the hook home! Man, what a rush! The fish immediately made a beeline for the bottom, on the bay side of the underwater ridge, and I got my first taste of the mano a mano battle that is fishing from a bridge. I already knew that the object of having fifty pound test mono on your reel, and a tight drag, was that you didn't want to let the fish get to running around the pilings, or anything else it could find, like the ice breaker poles, so I leaned back as hard as I could. I wanted to get that fish's head turned around and headed back up, or at least moving out from the bridge with the current. After a tense standoff, with the fish taking some drag, it finally moved downtide away from the bridge and I started pumping the rod, short and hard, working it toward the surface.

It finally came up, a ways off the bridge, and I got my first look at it, but only for a moment as it turned sideways, before diving straight back down and heading back toward the bridge. From my standpoint, it looked like a good fish, but I didn't have much time to dwell on it because it was headed straight back at the bridge, and fast. I was cranking in line like crazy, sweating bullets, hoping that this fish didn't just disappear under the bridge. I cranked and leaned as hard as I could, and fortunately got the fish up to the surface just as it got to the bridge. It thrashed around on the surface, still pretty green, and tried to make for the bottom again, but I hung on and thumbed the spool so that no drag was let out. The thrashing grew less.

I flipped my reel into free-spool and lightly thumbed the spool, letting the tiring fish swim away from the bridge with the current. It was a good fish, and now came the really difficult part, the scary part. After the fish was a safe distance from the bridge, I put the reel back in gear, and immediately felt the weight of the fish again. It was still pretty lively. I started working my way down toward the end of the bridge, but didn't get very far before I ran into an obstacle I had never planned for before. A light pole.

I had to pass my rod, with an active fish on the other end, around the outside of the street light that stood in the way of me and the end of the bridge. I didn't dwell on it too long, I just grabbed the rod above the reel with my right hand, and slid the butt of the rod around the outside of the pole until I could grab it with my left hand, then pulled it over the railing. You just had to make sure you didn't drop it. After doing it four or five hundred times, it became automatic.

After I got around the street light, I quickly, like almost ran to the end of the bridge, which wasn't very far. The bass was cooperating nicely, so as I was reaching the end of the bridge, I put my reel in free-spool again and let some line out, while making sure to keep good tension on the spool with my thumb. I didn't want the bucktail dropping out of the fish's mouth. I got to the fence and quickly did the one-handed hop, put the reel in gear, and made my way to the rocks and stopped. I looked down the slope of rocks and replayed the series of steps embedded in my memory. My gauntlet awaited me, beckoned to me, and it was time for me to accept the challenge.

I started down the rocks, focusing on keeping the line tight and keeping an eye on the fish. The last thing you want when you're going down the rocks is to have your fish make a dash to the bridge. If that happens, and you don't catch it in time, you are literally between a rock and hard place. I worked from rock, to rock, to rock, keeping my focus and taking my time. To be honest, I was crapping a brick, but it was going really well, so I just kept going, in that kind of numb, excited, focused, state of mind, until I stepped onto the landing rock. I was pretty relieved at that point, I can tell you that. So all that was left was to work this fish in, and get my thumb in its jaw. It didn't take long, nothing eventful.

I pulled the fish up on the rock and kind of sat down on my butt with the fish between my legs. The tail was still in the water, but that didn't matter to me, I had my clutches on my first bridge fish. My rod was unceremoniously lying on the rocks as I popped the bucktail out of the fish's mouth and tossed it aside. I then dragged it fully onto the rock to get a good look at it. I'm guessing it was about thirty-eight inches in length, but this is what my memory tells me, and while the chronology of my life is not great, this night has always been etched in my memory. It was a special night.

After thanking the fish for playing, I summarily revived and released the fish. I rarely keep striped bass, and those that I do are usually damaged beyond survival. So after releasing the fish, I sat down on a rock and stared out at the dark water. I felt exhilarated, I mean, the rush was undeniable, but as I sat there, I also felt sort of a sense of calm, like I had walked a long road and arrived at my destination. I don't know, it's kind of hard to explain. But most of all, I felt really, really, REALLY good, and that I couldn't wait to do it again.

Looking back on that night, and the hundreds of others that followed, I can't help but be struck by the fact that it all came down to chance, a random chain of events, and that any alteration or variation in that chain of events, would have resulted in that night and the hundreds of others that followed, having never happened. That entire chunk of my life came down to me throwing my twenty dollar entry fee into the Thursday night A-Class 9-Ball Tournament at Mr. Cue's Billiards. I drew the left bracket, same as Billy. Had either I, or Billy, drawn the right bracket, the chain would have been broken. Billy's first round match was directly beneath mine, in the same pairing bracket. If we each won our first rounds, we would face each other in round two. If either of us lost our first rounds, then the chain would have been broken. If Billy, or I, had drawn a different position in the left bracket, then again, the chain would have been broken.

But as fate would have it, we each won our first round and were in the middle of playing each other in the second round. Billy had won the last game, but had failed to drop any balls on his subsequent break. Had he not muttered something about fishing on his way back to his chair, then the final link in the chain of events would have been broken. But he did mutter something about fishing, and that single point in time, like a chemical reagent, ignited the process that inexorably lead to that first night, the hundreds of nights that followed, and everything else in my life that spun off of it. I'm probably just beating a dead horse here, but it really is strange when you look down the barrel of time to see exactly when it was that the trigger got pulled.

So looking back on the decades that I fished on and around the west end bridges, particularly the Wantagh bridges, several key realizations kind of come to the surface, out of the blur of memories from that time span. And when I say blur of memories, I mean a literal blur, because during the spring and fall seasons, I would fish every night, incoming or outgoing tides, until the tide died, or until dawn and the bite died. I ran on little sleep, and a lot of caffeine. Regardless, certain trends, events, and observations still remain intact to this day.

After the moratorium, when the stock rebuilding really got its mojo going in the mid to late 90s, word was getting out about fishing on the bridges, particularly the Wantagh bridges. The 3rd Wantagh Bridge became the focal point of this new interest simply because of the prodigious number of bass that took up residence there each season. Most newcomers thought it was just going to be easy pickings, and of course, they were dead wrong. For every eager new face that I would see walking out on the bridge for the first time, I would always think about what Billy said to me the first time he took me out on the 3rd, and sometimes I would almost be standing in the exact same spot as my first night out there, when I did. "Well, it's this simple. If you want to cash in on the riches these bridges have to offer, then there's a price you're gonna have to pay. The question is, are you willing to pay that price, because if it were that easy, everyone would be doing it, right?"

Billy was not wrong about this. It took me years, many years, over a decade, before I felt I truly had a handle on the bridges, and to be honest, there weren't a lot of people who could say the same. And you never stopped learning. There was always something more to learn, something that made you go WTF? The bridges were fascinating, challenging, scary, seductive, at times almost mystical, but when you learned them, understood them, nowhere, and I mean nowhere, could produce more fish, and bigger fish, on a consistent basis than the west end bridges. But the bridges didn't give them up for free. You had to pay the Piper.

One of the words I left out when describing the bridges in the last paragraph was humiliating. The first fall season I fished the 3rd Wantagh Bridge, when I caught my first bridge bass, I was using an eight foot rod and reel, that I already owned, that was not typical for fishing the bridges. In a word, the rod was too short. The ideal length for a bridge rod was nine foot, six inches. The reasoning for this is that when fishing into the tide, if a bass ran under the bridge, which they all did, your rod tip would extend far enough past the concrete of the bridge, so that your line would not rub on the concrete, thereby fraying your line, and potentially snapping you off. I was fishing the downtide side of the bridge and loop casting under the bridge, so it didn't matter to me my first time.

But after learning what the proper rod size was, I had one made for me at one of the bait and tackle shops in the west end area, I think it was Garan's B&T, but I can't say for sure, during the winter. So come spring, I had my brand new special bridge rod, which to be honest, was not at all what I expected. The butt was much longer than I was used to, so trying to loop cast with it was awkward. So I walked out onto the 3rd and took a couple casts at the second span. I was having trouble with the mechanics of the cast and consequently, I bounced bottom and picked up some crap on my bucktail hook. I cleaned it off as I walked to the third span, my favorite ridge, and made a loop cast back under the bridge.

My rod is pointed down as my bucktail touches down, and as I'm putting the reel in gear to my surprise, I get hit! I only have my right hand under the reel seat as I yank the rod up, which is too far out in front of me, and it slips out of my wet hands, the rod butt goes clank on the top rail of the railing, and the rod shoots straight down into the water. It was one of those moments where even a long string of curse words failed me. I just stood there in stunned silence before turning and walking back to my car and going home. That's one slow motion memory I could do without.

The next afternoon I said screw that, I went over to the large, now defunct, sporting goods store on Route 110 in Melville, might have even been Farmingdale, I think it was called Edelman's, and bought a new rod. That rod broke the mold for what was considered the traditional bridge rod, the nine foot, six inch, modified surf rod. The rod I bought was basically an eight foot graphite pool cue with a conventional reel seat and some line guides attached. I'm not sure what kind of fishing that rod was intended for, maybe hoisting tilefish up in three hundred feet of water, maybe even tuna fishing, but it fit the strategy for bridge fishing that I was putting together in my head. In the future I came to refer to that rod as the "Big Dog".

I've never been one to follow the crowd, so to speak. I've always been very analytical in most everything I do in life, and my fishing career did not escape that same scrutiny. Over the years I developed my own paradigm on how I fished the bridges, and the Big Dog played an important role in that process. Sounds really intellectual right? Well, it's really just a fancy way of saying I didn't believe in giving the fish an inch if I could help it. I reduced the fight down to three variables, either the rod breaks, the line breaks, or the hook bends out. Early on,

I started molding my own lead heads in modified molds for extremely heavy hooks, so that eliminated the hook bending out variable, so that left only the rod and line breaking variables to chance.

The concept was simple. When fishing downtide, the object was to get any large fish to move off the bridge with the tide. If they ran into the bridge against the current, then it was time to lean on them with the Big Dog. I would crank and lift as fast as possible, the goal of which was to get the fishes head as close to the surface as possible before it reached the bridge. When it did, then I would go into lockdown mode, reel the rod tip down really fast, jam my thumb into the spool to prevent line from leaking out of the already locked down drag, and then lift with all my might. Often, I would wind up with my rod on the top rail of the railing, my left hand pulling on the rod shaft, and the butt tucked under my right armpit, with me putting all my weight on it!

This was usually a sufficient enough deterrent to discourage the fish from trying to buck the tide any further, and typically it got them turned around and headed back out with the current, away from the bridge, where the battle could be concluded. It wasn't quite that easy when fishing into the tide, but the bridges I tended to fish into the tide on had pretty good clearance, and being a tall person with long arms helped to make up the eighteen inches I was missing off the length of my rod. So did getting down on my knees and fighting through the middle rail of the railing when necessary. But it was always the same strategy, either the line breaks or the rod breaks, and while I had lines pop from stress, or rub

125

against the concrete of the bridge until they frayed and snapped, the Big Dog, despite being ground on railings and concrete, tortured and beat to crap, lives on to this day.

In the decades I fished the bridges, I was always a loner, and I maintained kind of an outer orbit in relation to Billy. I tended to fish the Wantagh bridges the bulk of my time, and that's where I would run into Billy a lot. Billy tended to fish the front bridges more because they gave him a shot at those bigger fish he hunted nightly. But if the big fish didn't show on any given night, then he would usually wind up at the 3rd Wantagh, and when he did, he frequently had his sidekick Jeff with him. Jeff occupied a close inner orbit to Billy and was one of the first people I met on the bridges. Initially, we didn't interact very much at all, as Jeff tended to stay near Billy while fishing, while I tended to move around all over the bridge. I was very intense back then, a big guy with a Rangers cap, long pony tail, Fu Manchu mustache, and six pocket camo pants, so I'm not sure he knew what to make of me.

In the peak years, when Billy and I went to work on the 3rd Wantagh, it was something to see. We'd leap-frog all over the bridge, pulling one good fish after another, while the newcomers, and not-so-newcomers, just watched in awe. Those who frequented the bridge at that time, knew what to expect and enjoyed the show. They would ask questions and talk with us when we took a break for a smoke, or mid-tide when we gave our arms a break and let the fish reset for twenty minutes or so.

Somewhere around 2K, when the first waves of smaller fish started mixing in with bigger fish around the bridges, there were so many fish on the 3rd, I couldn't imagine what the bottom must have looked like. One night, I pulled seven fish, on seven straight casts, off one tiny little ridge way back up under one of the spans, just left of the center of the bridge. Seven straight casts to the exact same spot! They must have been gill to gill! The whole bridge was like that! There were nights where Billy and I would do over one hundred fish between the two of us, and just stop because our arms and legs were shot. Except I would always run down to the first span, Double Ridge Big Rock, to see if there was a really big fish laying behind the rock, before calling it a night.

Jeff turned out to be a really nice guy, kind of quiet and reserved. And one of my first interactions with him involved something that nice guys do for other bridge fishermen, that being, after walking my fish down, he offered to hold my rod and keep my fish under control, while I jumped the fence, and went down the rocks to unhook it. It's mutually beneficial. He gets to fight my fish a little bit, I get an easy trip down the rocks, he guides the fish to me, fish goes back quick and easy.

It all went well, I came back up the rocks, returned to get my rod and thanked him for his assistance. He handed me the Big Dog.

"Wow, this rod really has a lot of backbone!" he said.

"Yes it does," I nodded.

"Do you like this rod?" he asked.

"Yes I do."

"We use rods like this," he said, and proceeded to show me his prototypical bridge rod.

"I know," I replied. "I used to own one, but I lost it."

"You lost it, what happened?"

I pointed down toward the third span of the bridge.

"It's down there somewhere," I said flatly.

"You dropped it over the side of the bridge!" he exclaimed.

"Yup"

"Oh man, that sucks!"

"Yeah, that was pretty much what I was thinking when it happened… Anyway, thanks again for holding my rod for me, I appreciate it." And with that I went off to continue fishing, still fairly certain that Jeff didn't know what to make of me yet.

The Hat Trick

One night I arrived at the 3rd Wantagh expecting to find the beginning of the outgoing, but the current was still creeping in when I walked out on to the bridge. I noticed two guys I had never seen before down on my landing rock, with their little spinning rods, no doubt trying their hand at catching the plentiful bass they had heard inhabited the bridge. I walked to the first span, "Double Ridge Big Rock", my favorite on the incoming, unhooked my bait-tail, and lobbed a short cast out in front of me, letting the current sweep the jig under the bridge and over the ridge, where it stalled. I flicked the line with my thumb to give the jig a little life and bang, got slammed immediately.

I dragged her out unceremoniously, from under the bridge and down to the end, hopped the fence and danced down the rocks, to the wide-open eyes of the two guys on my landing rock.

"Make a hole," I said, as I came down fast. I dragged the fish in and quickly released it. It was in the low twenties. I ran back up, made another cast, and immediately hooked up again, dragged the fish out, and made my way down to the end. This time one of the guys called up and asked if he could release it. I gave him the thumbs up, as the tide was fading fast.

After he released it, I said, "Now for the hat trick." I made my cast and as soon as my jig bumped over the ridge, I got slammed again. This fish was bigger than the other two, mid-twenty, so I walked it down, waved off the help from below, and ran down the rocks. After releasing the fish, one of the guys said, "I heard it was easy to catch bass from these bridges!" I thought about everything I had gone through all those years and said, "Believe me, it ain't that easy." I went up the rocks, got in my car, and went to the D&D to wait out the tide change.

The second person I met and had any kind of relationship with on the bridges was a guy named John. I ran across him when I started making my first forays up onto the 2nd Wantagh Bridge. John was older than me, one of the original bridge fishermen, and was not what you would call a friendly person. He was like a dog that had marked his territory and didn't like trespassers, and he wasn't shy about letting you know. Every time I would squeeze by on the walkway, there would be lots of loud grumblings and curses. This went on for several nights over several weeks until I finally told him to get over it and get used to me, because I wasn't going anywhere. More grumbling, cursing, and bs about me having no business being on the bridge.

But the grumbling stopped, and over the next couple seasons we minded our own business when our paths crossed on the Wantaghs. Then one night on the 2nd Wantagh during the incoming tide, the fish were lined up on the whole length of the north side ridge, and these were all good fish, low to mid-twenties, with some upper-twenties thrown in for good measure. John and I were the only ones there, and we were hooking up one fish after another. As fast as one of us released a fish, the other would be walking one down. Sometimes we would both be hooked up, and had to wait for the other to release their fish before we could climb down and release ours. At that point, we still hadn't said a word to each other since I told him to get over himself.

This one night, I had walked a fish down and I'm standing a little way off the end of the bridge and I'm watching John release his fish, waiting for him to clear out, so I can hop the fence and get down to release mine. He pops the hook and sends his fish off, and then to my complete surprise, he waves me over to release my fish! I couldn't believe what I was seeing! I quickly walked the fish within range and he expertly released it, and made his way up the rocks. I reeled in my bucktail and stood there dumbfounded, not quite sure what I was going to say when he passed by me. I don't really remember the exact words, but it was your basic, "Thanks man", "No problem" exchange.

Obviously, I made sure to release his fish the first opportunity that arose, which didn't take long seeing as the bite was so hot. The releasing of each other's fish was almost like the passing of the peace pipe, a ceasing of hostilities between us, or maybe he just simply accepted the fact that I wasn't going anywhere after all. After that time we acknowledged each other's presence when our paths crossed with the usual, "Hey" or, "What's up" greeting, and eventually I got around to asking him what his name was.

Over time we began to talk, compare notes, and exchange information. But he could still be a hard ass about certain things, that was just the way he was wired. There came a time when I finally had to have my knee scoped. I had been living with a torn meniscus for over a year, but very early in October, I really tore it up climbing back up the rocks at the 3rd Wantagh Bridge one night. That side-lined me, so I called the orthopedic surgeon and asked if he could fit me in right away. As luck would have it, he had an opening somewhere around ten days down the road, I don't remember exactly when, but only if I could get the MRI done in time, which I did. The short version is I got my knee scoped, went home in a soft cast and crutches, and the doctor's orders not to mess up his good work. I wasn't sure what that meant, so eight nights later I headed out to the bridges.

The tide was incoming, so the 2nd Wantagh was my bridge of choice. I figured because it had the walkway, with the concrete divider wall on the road side of the walkway, I could walk a fish down right into the rocks, reel up tight, and then stick my rod into the base of the concrete divider wall and let my rod hang over the top rail of the railing. This way, all I had to do was figure out how to get over the fence and down the rocks on basically one leg. Not the most elegant way to land a fish, but probably workable considering the circumstances.

When I walked out onto the bridge, I wasn't surprised to see John, bent over, into a fish. It was another night where the fish were lined up on the north ridge, but there were some bigger fish that night. While John walked his fish down, descended the rocks and unhooked his fish, I had taken up position on the north side, and on my second cast hooked a really good fish. By the time I got my fish under control and was starting to limp my way down toward the end of the bridge, John came up. He paid no attention to the thirty or so pound bass thrashing in the water below.

"Where you been hiding, and what's with the gimp? he asked.

"I just got my knee scoped eight days ago."

"Then WTF are you doing up here!" he yelled.

"Hey man, I haven't fished since the beginning of the month, I'm going stir crazy!"

"Yeah, well you got no business being up here right now," he insisted.

I was starting to get annoyed, and I wanted to get this fish landed.

"John, can you do me a favor and hold my rod for me while I go down and get this fish?" I asked as nicely as I could.

"No," he said. "If you can't handle the bridge, you shouldn't be up here."

At this point my throbbing knee and the thrashing fish tipped my patience meter into the red. "C'mon John, save the king of the bridge BS for somebody that hasn't heard it before," I yelled, "it's a big fish, just let me get it back in the water, I won't ask you again the rest of the night, just hold my damn rod for me, what's the big f'ing deal?"

"All right!" he yelled, "just this one time, but don't ask me again!"

"Don't worry, I won't!"

I walked the fish down the rest of the way, John grumbling under his breath all the way, but he held my rod for me. I flopped over the fence and crabbed down the rocks. John led the fish over to me and I released it without incident. I then managed to crawl back up the rocks and flop back over the fence, my knee not being very happy about all of this. I limped over to John and thanked him for holding my rod and was told I was an idiot for my trouble. I just laughed, shook my head and went back to fishing.

As it turned out, the method of wedging my rod between the base of the concrete divider wall and the top rail of the railing proved to be effective in landing fish, but the flopping over the fence and trips up and down the rocks took their toll quickly. I caught several more fish before the pain in my knee sent me packing. But while I was there, every time we would squeeze by one another, John would mutter something like, "You're an idiot", or, "Go home stupid." He was a friend, but like I said, he could be a hard ass about certain things, that was just the way he was wired.

John was quite a character for sure, gruff and surly to the core. Other than me, the only other fishermen I saw in his orbit were two young brothers I referred to as the Nazi twins. Either one or both of them would occasionally show up on the 2nd Wantagh bridge when John was fishing it, but never by themselves. As you can tell by the nickname, I didn't like them very much. They were a couple of nasty, entitled, John wannabes, and to put it politely, I wound up having words with one of them one night, but John interceded while I was trying to decide if I should throw his scrawny ass off the bridge. They too, eventually got used to my presence, probably because of John's influence, even though they weren't around that much, and eventually disappeared from the bridge fishing scene altogether. Maybe they got caught robbing a bank or something.

But the single most important impact that John had on me, and my bridge fishing technique, had to be the bait-tail jig. I had started to experiment with jig configurations other than the standard bucktail and #70

Uncle Josh pork rind trailer combo, and one night on the 2nd I was showing John something new I was fishing with. It was my latest invention, a cut off rubber eel tail stuck onto a bullet head jig that I had cut the feathers off of, and had knocked the white paint off of. I had been catching a lot of fish on it, so I was kind of cocky and wanted to show off.

John looked at it, held it up in front of him for a second.

"It's ass heavy," he said. "The jig head is not balanced." He handed my creation back to me. My cocky attitude took a punch in the face.

"What do mean it's not balanced?" I asked.

"What part of not balanced don't you understand... hold the f'ing thing up and look at it," he demanded. "It hangs down in the back, it'll swim like an eel with a lead turd in its ass. You'll catch fish on it for a while, but they'll figure it out and stop hitting it... it looks wrong."

John had his line and jig hanging over the side of the bridge, down near the water and out of my line of sight. He proceeded to reel his line in and showed me what he had tied to the end of his line. He held it up for me to see. It was the essence of simplicity.

"This is what you want to be using." he said.

I stared at it for a few seconds as it dangled from his hand. I had never seen a jig like that before.

"What is that?" I asked.

"It's a bait-tail." he replied.

The lead head was shaped like a long slender bullet and the eyelet was located in the middle of the head, so the whole jig hung at ninety degrees to the fishing line.

And instead of bucktail tied to the hook, it had a perfectly sized piece of surgical tubing, about five inches long, fitted to the back of the head, that was gradually taper cut on top, from just before the hook bend to the end of the tubing, and then cut on the bottom, straight down the middle, right back up to the hook bend. This allowed those two, thin, tapered sections of tubing to flutter in the current and provide swimming motion to the jig, all in a perfect horizontal, balanced, presentation.

"Wow, bait-tail, huh… where can I get them?" I asked.

John just laughed a little. As a matter of fact, I think that's the only time I ever heard him laugh. I always assumed I would have had to fall down the rocks and break my neck to get him to laugh.

"You can't get them anywhere," he said. "You have to make them yourself."

"Well, then where can I buy the jig heads or— "

"Did you hear what I said! You have to make them yourself… now I've shown you enough already, go fish your constipated eel and don't waste any more of my time!"

Always the charmer John was, but I have him to thank for turning me on to bait-tails. This is another case of how happenstance created a chain of events, a nexus if you will, that ultimately had a profound effect on my life. After he showed me his bait-tail, a fire was lit under my ass and I dove straight into the jig molding craft that I mentioned earlier in this book. I won't rehash that episode, other than to say I went way overboard with it. Typical me.

One other thing about John. John hated Billy, couldn't stand him, the mere mention of his name would set him off. I never figured out what that was all about other than it must have been something that went way back to the beginnings of the west end bridge fishing story. Billy, as far as I know, doesn't know what it was about either, and he can comment on his feelings on John if he wants to. The only thing Billy has said repeatedly to me about John, is that John was a great fisherman, that despite all of the BS, John was a really good fisherman. It's my understanding that John passed on a while back, so I'll just leave this here. He was grumpy on a good day, mean as a snake on a bad day, but he was okay in my book. RIP.

Billy   caught this sixty-three pound bass and four other fish over fifty pounds in one amazing night on the Meadowbrook Bridge.

Big Fish…

When it comes to fishing for striped bass, there's a reason so few people have caught striped bass over fifty pounds. Obviously, there simply aren't as many of them around, as there are the lesser weight classes. That's a given, but there is another, less obvious reason that few fishermen realize. Big striped bass, those upper forty, fifty pound, and over fifty pound fish, are a completely different animal from their younger, smaller sisters and brothers. Their behavior and habits are different from smaller fish, and because of this, they remain an enigma to most fishermen, surf, boat, or otherwise. Note, I said most.

There was a charter boat captain out in Montauk years back who developed quite a reputation for catching big bass trolling his out-sized bunker spoons. He knew when, he knew where, and he knew how, and he racked up some pretty good numbers along the way. Was trolling bunker spoons considered cheating? I don't think so, but some fishermen did. I remember the griping about him, guys saying what's so hard about dragging those stupid spoons behind a boat, and things like that. First off, he made those spoons, and I'm amazed he could even get them to swim at the right depth, but most of all, he was able to repeat his results over and over again. That was the mark that he understood big fish behavior!

I might have tipped my hand on where this is headed, so I'll just charge forward. Being involved in the New York and Long Island fishing scene for many years, I know a lot of very excellent surf fishermen, some of the best. But I would be lying if I said I hadn't hear some talk through the years, about how catching big fish from a bridge is somehow cheating. If you've made it this far into the book, then you probably have some idea of what was involved in fishing from those bridges. I won't belabor the point, but catching big fish from a bridge is no more cheating than dragging bunker spoons through the rips, or fishing from a pier, or the rocks of an inlet. Simply put, Billy has caught more fifty pound striped bass than anybody else, period, and to use his own words, "if it were that easy, everyone would be doing it, right?"

Rich: I just finished writing a section about Grumpy John and I mentioned how he hated your guts.

Billy: [*laughs*]

Rich: What was that all about anyway?

Billy: I'll be honest with you, I really don't know. He just didn't like me. John kind of felt like he owned the bridges… he hated everybody and the feeling was mutual. I'm surprised you got along with him.

Rich: [*laughing*] I didn't give him much choice.

Billy: I'll tell you what though. He may have been an asshole, but he was a really good fisherman. He knew those bridges and caught a lot of fish in his day, and a lot of big fish. I got a good story about John for you. Kevin told me this one. You know, nobody really fished the 3rd Wantagh on the incoming, it was mostly considered an outgoing tide bridge.

Rich: I used to.

Billy: Yeah, well so did John. So anyway, Joe and Kevin come over the bridge in Kevin's truck and they see John down in the southwest corner of the bridge. They slow down for a drive by and they see John bent over the top rail and his rod is bent down to the water. Kevin wanted to pull over because he thought that John had a good fish on, but Joe was like, "Screw John, that prick, he's probably just snagged on the bottom," so they decided to keep going. Turns out that John had four big fish that night, a high forty and three fifties. Kevin was so pissed off that he listened to Joe. [*laughs*]

Rich: [*laughing*]… Not surprised it was the southwest corner though. Every big fish I caught on the 3rd came

141

from there. Either from the hole between the two ridges on the incoming, or behind the big rock on the outgoing. But the Wantaghs didn't hold a lot of really big fish.

Billy: No, they held a ton of fish, more than any of the other bridges by far, but not a lot of fifties. I'll tell you that without a doubt, the two bridges that held the most big fish, were the Meadowbrook (aka Big M) and the Swift Creek. That's where most of my big fish came from.

Rich: I still can't get over the Swift Creek. I drove over that bridge so many times on my way to the Meadowbrook and never gave it a second thought.

Billy: Nobody did, nobody ever fished that bridge, and I caught so many big fish on that bridge, but only on the incoming. You know, big fish do what big fish want to do. You been doing this long enough, you know this already, but big fish don't mix with smaller fish. A pod of big fish may show up in the middle of a bunch of smaller fish, but they don't hang around with them, or travel with them, nothing like that. They're different, and you have to realize that if you want to catch them. Like that week in 1991, when I had all those fifties on the Meadowbrook.

Rich: Yeah, which week was that... you've had more than a few of them.

Billy: [*laughs*] OK, that one week, it was November 19th, it was an amazing thing to see, listen, we (Billy, Jeff, and

142

a few others in Billy's orbit) had been fishing the bridge, and we had a good bite, no gigantic fish, but tons of those twenty to thirty pound fish. So we were going through them, and about a week before the 19th, it drops dead, the bait left, the fish left, there was nothing on the bridge, you know like when the fish leave after a moon, there's nothing there. So I remember talking to Jeff and saying that there isn't a chance that this is over, and everyone thought it was over, the regular bridge guys were like "eh, it's over", because it's late in the year already, you know.

So I go up every night, for like five straight nights, and there are no fish on the bridge. I picked a few small fish off the bottom, but there were no fish on top, no bait on top, nothing. I walked all the bridges looking for fish, I'm thinking there's got to be some fish somewhere, there's no way this is over, the waters still too warm. Jeff had already quit, he had stopped coming up with me, I had been fishing three or four days on my own, he hadn't come up at all, and there was no one on the bridges, and I'm like, there isn't a chance that this is over, I was sure of it, there was no way.

So I'm looking and looking, and on the week of the 19th, I go up, and that first night I go up, there's like three or four good fish on the bridge, all by themselves, and they were on the north side, not on the south side. In that week, if I'm not mistaken, I think I caught seven fish over fifty pounds, and a lot of forty pound fish. And it was a building bite, and what I mean by that is that every night I went up, there were more fish, and bigger fish.

Like the first night there were those four fish on the bridge, of which I caught two of them, then that was it for that night. So, the next night I went up, I didn't tell Jeff by the way, because he didn't come up with me, so I was kind of punishing him a little bit…

Rich: [*laughing*]

Billy: [*laughs*] I used to do that, like, you don't want to come up, you don't deserve to know what's here… maybe you shouldn't put that in the book… Anyway, I was amazed, I was all by myself, there was no one up there, it was a late tide, and I'm thinking this is great, big fish. And each night there were more and more big fish. One night I had two fifties and two forties, it was all big fish, there were no thirties at all. Man my heart is pumping because I have all these fish to myself. The night I caught all those fifties was the last night of the bite, and I had told Jeff to come on up. While heading up, there were a couple guys on the Loop Parkway Bridge, so I flew over to the Meadowbrook; cause I didn't want anybody to see me.

I came out on the Meadowbrook Bridge and it was lined with big fish, I mean lined with big fish, from the shore to the first light, you know that span, it's like what, maybe one hundred feet at the most? There were six or seven enormous fish sitting right in the shadow line, and these things are obviously feeding aggressively. Like I always

144

say, big bass are easy to catch, they're just hard to find, sometimes they're as easy to catch as snappers for Christ's sake. On my very first cast I caught a fifty pound bass. I dragged his ass down to the shore, got down as fast as I could, threw'em back up under the bridge and I ran back out. When I ran back out, there was one of that bunch of six or seven left in the shadow line, and I got him! I literally surfed him into shore, flew down the rocks, measured him out and got'em back in the water in record time. Man, I couldn't move fast enough at that point.

I ran back out, and the entire bridge on the south side, all the way out to the center span, was lined with big fish feeding. And as fast as you threw a bucktail in, you had a fish on. I had four fifties that night, It was amazing! I have never seen striped bass feeding as aggressively as they did that night. And the next day, this is good, there was a tackle shop that had just opened up. I think it used to be called Charlie's Bait and Tackle, a guy named Charlie Schaffer owned it. Well, he either died or sold it, and this guy Shelly, he was just a businessman, he wasn't really a fisherman, and he bought it, and I went in there when he first bought it and I liked him, we got along real good, so I helped him out, you know what I mean.

So I weighed my fish in there, and when I got in there in the morning, the whole world knew about it already. It was amazing, that guy Eric that used to own Finstrike, he came up and said to me, "Greek, you had to be the guy that caught those four fifties, right?" I said, "Yeah, why?" He says, "We heard that in Pennsylvania." I said, "I didn't

145

even tell anybody yet!" [*laughing*] Man… I mean this was before the Internet, you know! I don't know how word got out on it so fast, but boy, did it travel [*laughs*]

Rich: [*laughing*]

Billy: And everyone knew, everyone was calling everyone, they said it was some guy with a big mustache, so they knew it was me. And I got to be honest with you, in all the years I've fished, that was the most aggressive bite I've ever seen with big fish, in my life. They were lined up, right on top, nose touching the line, and there were dozens of them, and none of them were under fifty pounds. And it's a shame, because you can only get a big fish in so fast, you know, and I was like super pumped, I was so excited, I was like dragging these fish to shore, and the whole thing didn't last much more than an hour, and then that was it, they left. I knew then it was over.

And everybody heard about it, and I never forgot, because I had talked to Fred Golofaro from the Fisherman, like a day or two later… I didn't go up the next night by the way, Jeff went back up and wanted me to go. I said, "I'm not going." He said, "Why not!" I said, "It's over, when big fish feed that aggressively, that intensely, that's it, it's their last feed before they migrate." There was like a hundred guys on the bridge the next night, there wasn't a fish on the bridge. And probably half of them thought I was full of sh!t, because by the time they showed up, there was nothing left. I think I had seven or eight fifty pound fish, you know. I'm sure of the date though.

And you know, it's amazing, what I really remember, when you catch those really big fish on a strong tide, they go under the bridge right away. I mean, you know this, you've fished for them, they go under the bridge, and then they stop, and they turn and go forward slowly into the tide. When they do that, the line screams, like it was a hundred mile an hour wind, it makes that whining sound, like [*makes a sound like wood being cut by a power saw*] because they're going back up into the tide to release the pressure on them. That to me was really exciting, man, I really miss that, it's a shame they took our bridges away and we're not allowed to fish them anymore, because there's not a whole lot in my life of fishing that gets my heart pumping more than catching big fish on top of those bridges. You know, I don't get that when I'm in the boat.

Rich: Yeah… I mean, why would you, there's not that risk of the fish being able to wrap you, or saw you off on anything. Basically, it's I got you, you're not going anywhere, so you're just waiting the fish out. But on a bridge, It's brute force and speed, I got to get you, before you get me.

Billy: You ain't kidding. You hook that big fish, there's been times in my life when I been on my hands and knees trying to pull that fish out from under the bridge, it's like holy crap, this things got horsepower. It all depends on the fish and the tide, some fish are built like a brick wall,

147

solid and heavy built, and on a moon tide, they can beat the sh!t out of you.

Here's another thing about catching fish from the bridges. When you first go out on a bridge and you look down at fish in the water, you don't know how big they are. And no matter how big you think they are, when you get them out of the water, they're way f'ing bigger than you thought, you know what I mean. I remember that one time when I had that fifty-nine pound fish, I never forgot that because there were three big fish, and the one in the middle was visibly much bigger, much bigger. They didn't look a lot longer, because I don't think bass get a lot longer, but this fish, if you're looking down, and the fish on the right and left are like five inches across, this fish was like nine inches across.

And they were tight fish, like they were inches apart, and when I brought that bucktail across that fish's face, the one on the right just darted out and grabbed it, and I got him instead. When I saw them, like in my mind, I was thinking, ah, this is probably two forties and a good fifty maybe. And when I hooked this fish, it blew under the bridge and slammed my rod into the bridge. He just took off under the bridge, and I was having trouble getting him out from under the bridge. I mean, I was really struggling. I remember thinking to myself, this fish is giving me a ton of sh!t for a forty pound fish, because I didn't think he was that big, you know, because you really can't tell just by looking.

148

I'm like, man this fish is beating me up, but then sometimes you think, okay, it's a moon, it's a strong tide, the fish got away from me a little bit. But when I got that fish to the shoreline, and pulled him out, I was like holy sh!t, this things huge! You just don't realize how big a fish is until you actually pull him out of the water. That's when you see the girth and size, because up until then, a fifty-two or fifty-three inch fish can be anywhere between fifty to seventy pounds, you know, and until you pull them out and see how thick they are, and how wide they are, you just don't know for sure. That fish was fifty-nine pounds... can you imagine what that middle fish must have weighed? I never forgot that because that fish in the middle was visibly much, much, bigger, you know.

Rich: It's always about the fish you didn't catch, right?

Billy: Yeah... But can you imagine how big that fish must have been!

Billy was always looking for opportunities to maximize his abilities to catch big fish on the bridges, and anything that stood in the way of his endeavors rankled him. Such was the case with the eight foot high chain link fences that bordered the bicycle path on the east side of the Wantagh bridges. Those fences prevented him from being able to fish the uptide shadow line of those bridges on the outgoing. But he just couldn't help torturing

149

himself, as he would climb up on them, straddle the top, and sit there looking for fish. And when big fish showed up, it drove him crazy.

At some point before I began fishing the bridges, Billy was down at the 3rd Wantagh along with another guy, later known to me as the Fireman. As usual, Billy couldn't resist crossing over the street to the east side of the bridge, to climb the fence and see if any big fish were in the shadow line. The Fireman went with him. They walked out to roughly the middle of the bridge, just before the ice breakers, and up the fence Billy went, assuming his patented leg-over straddle position. It only took a second for him to spot a giant bass up on top, nose on the line. This was more than Billy could take.

"Holy sh!t!" Billy yelled. "Give me my rod!" Billy shouted, gesturing to the Fireman to hand him his rod.

"What are you kidding?" asked the Fireman as he handed the rod up to Billy.

"Nope."

Before the Fireman could ask what he planned to do when he hooked the fish, Billy had fired off a cast and was leading his bucktail right across the face of the giant bass. The bucktail disappeared into its mouth. Billy reared back and set the hook, all this while perched atop a wobbling eight foot chain link fence. The bass immediately turned and bolted for the bridge and Billy started cranking.

"Uh-oh!" Billy muttered.

"Yeah, now you think about it!" the Fireman laughed. "C'mon, climb over, put your feet on my shoulders, hurry up!" "I'll walk you down, we'll see if we can land this thing."

Well that whole impulsive bit of enthusiasm had less than no chance of success, and it didn't take long for the bass to fray the line on the bottom of the bridge, pop the line, and swim off with a new piece of jewelry in its lip. Normally, if you fished the fence side of the Wantagh bridges, you did so from a bridge stand, something Billy had brainstormed up back in the day. Conceptually, the bridge stand was not unlike a tree stand for hunters, but unlike hunter's tree stands, which are commercially available, bridge stands were strictly a DIY project.

Basically, you hooked the base of the stand into the chain link of the fence and then the heavy wires, or chains connected to the back corners of the stand, were attached to the chain link near the top of the fence, so that the stand was level. You set it up so that when you climbed up onto it, the top of the fence was roughly waist high on you, and allowed you to bend over the top of the fence. Needless to say, keeping your feet from slipping was a priority.

Fishing from a bridge stand required at the very least, one necessary accessory, and that was a bridge gaff. This barbaric piece of equipment was also a DIY project. I made mine using three large shark hooks, a one and a half inch section of one inch wooden dowel, a screw eye, a dog leash clip, a ten ounce bank sinker, and a hundred foot length of one hundred pound braided nylon cord. I ground off the barbs on the shark hooks, and these were big hooks, and then cut grooves one hundred and twenty degrees apart, vertically, along the wooden dowel, so that the hook shanks fit into them. I then epoxied the hooks into the dowel, just below the hook eyes, effectively making a very large treble hook. I then pre-drilled and screwed the screw eye into the top of the dowel, and gave the dowel a coat of polyester resin for good measure. I tied the dog leash clip about one foot from the end of the braided cord and then tied the end of the braided cord to the screw eye. The sinker was then tie wrapped to the base of the treble hooks, before the bends, for ballast. The braided cord and bridge gaff went into a small bucket until ready for use.

The drill went like this. The bridge stand went up on the fence at your place of choice. You leaned your rod against the fence, put the bucket on the ground, pulled out the bridge gaff, reached up and hung it on the fence, and up you went to your perch. You picked up your rod and fished. When you hooked a fish, and if you managed to get it under control, you put the reel clicker on, thumbed the spool, threw it into free spool, pulled the rod in, grabbed the line with one hand, let your rod butt down to the ground with the other, then grabbed the bridge gaff, clipped the dog leash clip to your line, let the gaff slid down your line until the clip stops at your bucktail.

By then, you have already knocked the fish in the head with the gaff and it's usually registering its objection, but the hook should be under the fish's chin. You then start yanking up on the braided line, the object of which is to sink one of the shark hooks into the chin of the fish. It might take a couple of yanks, but you know when you hit home. Then it's just a matter of letting go of your fishing

152

line and hauling the whole mess, hand over hand, up the side of the bridge, over the top of the fence, and down to the ground.

Then, of course, you must climb down from the bridge stand, and get the fish unhooked before the untangling begins. Now, if you planned on keeping the fish, you could take your time untangling your fishing line from the gaff line, but if you wanted to release the fish, you had to shake a leg. This meant stretching your gaff line and fishing line out on the bicycle path and unwrapping your fishing line from the gaff line. Sometimes you were lucky and the fish didn't twist much on the way up and the breeze kept your line out of the way. Other times, not so lucky, and you wound up with a twisted mess.

Either way, you had to get the two lines separated, your line back on your reel, the gaff line back by the bucket, the gaff up on the fence, the fish up on the stand, and then you back up on the stand with the fish. From there you had to put one of the shark hooks through the thin skin in the fish's chin, maybe reuse the hole you brought him up on, lift the fish and the gaff over the top of the fence, and then let the fish slide back down to the water. A glove was useful in preventing rope burns. After that, usually all that was needed was to let go of the braided line and the ten ounce sinker would drop the gaff hook out of the fish's jaw, thereby releasing the fish.

If all this sounds difficult, you are correct, it was, particularly if you fished alone. But over time you got used to the mechanics and could manage the operation quickly. But the best way to fish from bridge stands was to do it with a partner. This saved a lot of headaches. When one guy hooked a fish, the other would immediately dismount and come over to assist. As soon as the hooker had his fish ready for gaffing, he would hand his rod to the partner, then the hooker could take care of gaffing his fish. Once the fish was gaffed and on its way up, the assistant would take a few steps away from the stand, holding the rod up by the fence top, and reel in the slack fishing line as the fish was brought up.

This helped reduce tangles and made it easier to clear the ones that ultimately did happen. He could also help getting the fish down to the bicycle path, or anything else needed. Partner fishing became desirable when fishing from bridge stands and as you'll soon learn, some interesting stories came about while fishing from them. The whole bridge stand thing died out over time, but I believe Billy still has his original bridge stand and I kept my bridge gaff, which saw use at the sixty-five foot Ponquoque Bridge out in Southampton many years later. But that's another story for another book.

Billy: I was in the dentist's office one day, I never forgot this, I'm sitting there and I'm flipping through some BS magazine, and I see a picture of a young girl, maybe fourteen, fifteen years old, something like that, and she's holding an enormous bass. The magazine wasn't a fishing magazine, it was just some BS article in some magazine, maybe a local Long Island rag, I don't know. And this had to be around… I'm thinking the very late 80s… and the fishing in the late 80s was tough, you know.

Rich: Yeah… definitely.

Billy: So I'm reading it, and this is how the article goes. It says, young girl was free dive spear fishing with her father in the State Boat Channel, and a school of huge fish, it didn't say striped bass, it said huge fish, swam over their head about twelve feet above them. Now you know my mind is reeling, because I know the State Boat Channel like the back of my hand, like how many places could you be on the bottom, and above you has twelve feet of water over your head, with a school of a hundred plus giant striped bass swimming over your head.

She said, as the school went by, she shot one of them, which she said was one of the average sized fish in the school, and she said there were fish much, much bigger than the one she shot. The one she shot and took the picture with was a fifty-seven pound fish, and the tail had smacked her in the nose and broke her nose, and her father helped her out and got the fish.

Rich: You know, I vaguely remember hearing something about this. I think I read about it in a Nick Karas' article in Newsday. He used to have a page in the sports section on Friday.

Billy: All I know is I was thinking to myself, there's a school of bass in high fifty pound plus class, with fish

155

much, much bigger swimming around, and no one knows about it? So I start doing research, I get all the fishing magazines, Nor'east [Saltwater], all of them, search all the reports for the year, nobody caught a fifty pound fish, no one. Not a hint of a big fish. These fish are going through the State Boat Channel and no one knows about it! Now I know that in the fall, some of the big fish exit Great South Bay through the State Boat Channel and go out through Jones Inlet, I found that out years ago when I used to fish the boat channel, which probably means they came in from Jones Inlet. Anyway, I was looking for these fish, and I couldn't find them, they didn't pop up anywhere. I mean think about, a school of fish that size that isn't feeding, you sit down to bait up, they could swim right past your boat and you'd never know it.

So, me and Shawn, on the 3rd Wantagh, it was June 10th on the outgoing tide, on the northeast side, we ran into those fish. The only fish I've ever come across that I couldn't stop, I couldn't stop one of them, not a one. Me and Shawn got smoked, I mean busted up bad. We lost like five or six bucktails a piece, I couldn't even slow those fish down, that was when we were still fishing from the bridge stands. I hooked up first, as soon as my bucktail went over that little hump on the north side, whack, I had him. This fish went so hard it slammed my rod into the bridge! Even with the drag tightened down, it just ripped line off, and my rod was bouncing off the bridge, I mean, I was starting to get worried about my rod it was taking such a beating. And then all of a sudden my line broke.

Then before I could even get the words out of my mouth, Shawn hooked up. He got smoked in short order, I mean we were losing a bucktail on every fish, and our line was getting destroyed on the bridge, and we never even slowed these fish down. They were so powerful, I've never felt anything like it. At one point, I actually ran back to my truck to get two new spools of line and swapped them out on the Squidders, but it really didn't matter, we just got brutalized by those fish, absolutely brutalized. I lost five fish, and I think Shawn lost four. We had to quit because we had nothing left to fish with. I mean, I would have really loved to have seen just one of them, just one.

Rich: Just out of curiosity, why didn't you cross the parkway and fish the big rocks on the downtide side of the bridge? They were right in line with the hump on the north side. Maybe some of those big fish had backed off and were hanging behind some of the other structure.

Billy: You know, that didn't even occur to me to do that! It was so intense, and we were getting destroyed by those fish so fast, it never even entered my mind.

Rich: So… June 10th you say.

Billy: June 10th.

Rich: June 10th is right about the time I lost my biggest fish on the 2nd.

157

Billy: Yeah, that's what I'm saying, I think those big fish have been there all the time, and we just didn't know about it.

Rich: Well that fish surprised the hell out of me, and broke my heart when I lost it, because it was my fault. It was a done deal and I blew it, you know. I've always felt that the 2nd held fewer fish than the 3rd Wantagh, but more bigger fish, you know what I mean?

Billy: I'd absolutely agree with that.

Rich: But I never expected anything the size of this fish, and I didn't expect to catch it where I did. I hooked it coming out from under the bridge, on the south side, just to the right of the last light, before you get to the big platform by the boat channel. There's a couple rocks down there, and it's pretty deep, you know the spot.

Billy: I do.

Rich: But most of my big fish on those bridges usually come near the bridge edges, not near the middle, so I was a bit surprised by this fish, and pretty happy it didn't just run me over to the ice breakers and wrap me up. I knew right away it was a big fish when I leaned on it and nothing happened, almost like it didn't even know it was hooked. It was weird, it just started moving straight off the bridge, downtide, and I did something I never, ever do. I backed off my drag and let her go. I mean, as far as

158

I was concerned, the farther away from the bridge she was, the better.

You know, I had been fishing the bridges for quite a while at this point, so I didn't get too worked up over bigger fish, but when I felt the power of this one, my mind started racing and the adrenalin really kicked in. I had to make some decisions, you know, because I wasn't in a great place. There was a guy in a boat who was slowly making his way in toward the bridge. I yelled out to him that I had a good fish on and that it was quite a ways out, and asked if he could back off for a few minutes until I got it under control. I guess he could see my line reflecting in the street light, because he pointed to it, took his boat out of gear, and drifted back with the tide for a bit. Man, was I glad of that!

Then I wanted to see if I could get her to the surface, to see what I was up against, so I tightened the drag and started to lean on her to see if the current would bring her up. It didn't work. She just turned and started steaming back toward the bridge, against the tide, but she was headed in to the left of the light pole, and I'm like, if I can't get around this light pole now, I'm f'd. So I quickly jammed the butt of my rod around the pole and grabbed it, and as I swung my rod around, I gave her that moment of slack… I'm lucky I didn't lose her right there, because it wasn't the most graceful maneuver I've ever executed. [*laughing*]

Bill: [laughs] Those light poles can be a pain in the ass sometimes.

Rich: Oh yeah. So I get around the pole and I'm reeling, and leaning, reeling, and leaning, and she's steaming toward the span, and I'm trying desperately to get her up to the surface, because I don't want her going deep into the bridge, you know. I figure if she goes in deep, I'm f'd. So she comes up into the span, right in the center of the span, and starts to go under the bridge, and I have no idea where she is in the water column, and you know it's pretty deep there, and I'm thinking *this is not good, this is not good.* All I know is that she's not on top, so I decide it's now or never. I lean over the rail and go full stop. The Big Dog bent further than it's ever bent before, and if that line had slipped through my fingers and thumb, I would've had blisters for weeks. And you know that sound you were talking about, that line makes under stress, when the current runs against it?

Billy: That screaming, whining, sound, yeah!

Rich: Well my line starts making that sound! I could feel the fish pulsing, I think it was starting to come up under the bridge in an arc. It was so intense, I mean, this was a whole new level of play. I've caught several upper forties, and this was not that… So we're locked in this kind of Mexican standoff, and it couldn't have been more than maybe ten or fifteen seconds, you know, but during that time my mind is going, what happens if she breaks for the pilings, what happens if she surfaces and starts thrashing around and spits the bit, what happens if… and then she simply turned around and bolted straight out, center span, with the current. So, I let her go again.

She was pretty cooperative from there on in. I watched the line on my reel get less and less as she thought she might just leave the area with the tide. After she was off the bridge a ways, I wanted to try and get her to the surface again, The guy in the boat had been very patient, and I wanted to get my first look at her. So I put the brakes on and started leaning on her, coaxing her up from the depths. She starting moving to my left, so I started working my way down toward the end of the bridge. I was definitely happy with that direction. She was now doing that fussy thing, you know, short lived burst runs, maybe one to the left, one to right, and so on, but she was coming up, and she was tiring, but she was still really strong, and just felt really heavy in the current, so I wasn't taking anything for granted.

Finally, I saw my line coming up, and I felt like Captain Ahab in Moby Dick "She breaches!" [laughing]… and I remember this clear as a bell. She was moving to my left, out a little further than I thought, and fairly close to the guy in the boat. She just glides up to the surface, full side view, leaning slightly away from me, so I get a pretty good look at her girth, and then thrashes in the water for a second or two, before diving back down. Even at that distance, I almost crapped my pants. The guy on the boat shouts "Holy Sh!t!" twice, and I have to snap out of my daze and get back to work.

This got long so I'll cut to the chase. I made the decision to work my way down the bridge, leaving the fish a fair way out. After getting around the other light pole I was committed, and I knew that if I decided to land this fish from the rocks, when it was still that far out, I ran the risk of her making a run at the bridge, in which case I would be f'd. I just wasn't sure I wanted to bring her in to the bridge and then walk her down for landing. On retrospect, I think that would have been the right move, but we all have twenty-twenty hindsight, right?

Billy: You bet.

Rich: So, I work the fish in close to rocks. The guy in the boat had kind of followed the fish in and was fairly close, he definitely wanted to see this fish. The fish was shot, I mean dead tired, not the way I normally like to deal with fish, but I had never caught anything this big before, and this fish was huge. I'm pumping her in to me and I'm thinking all kinds of happy thoughts, and I have this fish within about three rod lengths of the landing rock, The fish is on its side, and I can clearly see my bait-tail in its upper jaw. The top part of the bait-tail is actually out of the water, you know, and I drop my rod tip just a bit to take in some line, and I watch the bait-tail drop out of the fish's mouth.

Billy: Yeah… I remember you telling me about this… Sickening.

Rich: I mean I was stunned. How f'ing stupid could I be. I stood there and watched that beautiful giant fish, roll over on its back, go belly up, sink in a head first arc, and disappear in the current. The guy in the boat goes, "What happened?" I said, "I lost it." He says, "You what?" I told him I lost it, he couldn't believe it. To be honest, neither could I. I couldn't fish any more that night, I just left and went home.

Billy: Losing a big fish is the worst feeling in the world. It'll make you want to puke.

Rich: Yeah, well I'll tell you what. At that point, I had remained sober for a lot of years, and fishing was a large part of what helped to keep me sober. But on my way home, I passed one of the old gin mills I used to frequent back in my drinking days, and I'd be lying if I didn't say that I had an almost overpowering urge to pull in to the parking lot, go through the front door, pull up a stool at the bar, and dive head first off the wagon.

Billy: I'm glad you didn't. That would have been a mess. [*laughs*]

Rich: Brother, you ain't kidding.

Wanna Make A Bet!

Billy: I'm on a job one day, and the contractor is this guy named Jay. I'm the painter, he's the contractor. He's young, not young, young, he's like forty-five, in good shape, and somehow we get started talking about fishing. I guess he had done some fishing, I don't know, I wasn't really paying much attention. So he asks me where I fish and I tell him I'm a bridge fisherman, and he's like, "You fish from bridges?" And I say, "Yeah, there's a lot of fish up there, I often get one on the first cast." He says, "I doubt it." So now that he's called me out, we gotta go. So, I say, "You wanna bet!" He goes, "Yeah, what do you want to bet?" I say, "How about lunch tomorrow?" He goes, "You got it!"

So after work, we went right up to the Loop Parkway Bridge in his truck. I take my rod out, and walk out to that one piece, where that little hole is there, and on my very first cast I catch a bass. And he's not really impressed, you know, not like a lot of people who would be impressed with that, he's like, "OK, that was good." And the next day he buys me lunch. Then he goes, "Do you want to try it again tonight?" I said, "Sure." I go up, I get a fish right away. He buys me lunch again. So, about a week goes by, I figure he's had enough, you know. But out of nowhere, he comes up to me and says, "OK, how about tonight we go up?" I said, "Sure." I got a fish on the first cast. He goes, "OK, you win, show me how to do this!" [laughs]

164

Billy: So you know how they're always talking about big baits catching big fish?

Rich: Yeah, what about it.

Billy: Do you remember the big bucktails that were used by some of the guys back then?

Rich: No, not really, not unless you mean those things that looked like reverse parachute jigs I saw guys using a couple times. I mostly kept to myself.

Billy: Well… this guy John was making them back then, I think he called them Tarantulas. I kind of got some ideas off it. Like I made those three quarter ounce bucktails with the big 8/0 hooks with a ton of hair on them, so they didn't sink fast. They worked real good when there was a strong tide and the fish were right on top, they just swung perfectly into the line without sinking. And there were times when there was big bait around, and we made these big bucktails, they weren't heavy, they were just big.

So we would take a bucktail and groove the head just behind the eye, where you tie the line, and we'd tie bucktail hair in there. Then we'd tie a lot of bucktail hair onto a strong, short shank hook, then slide it over the bucktail hook with a little piece of rubber to keep it in place, basically a stinger hook on the bucktail. That gave you about eight inches of bucktail. Then instead of the #70 pork rind we normally use, I would get the big offshore pork rind and put that on, so the lure became about a foot and change.

But man, when bunker were around, big fish, they inhaled that, sometimes they would hit that so hard Rich, you would hook them in the back of the throat, not even in the mouth, you know what I mean, they pounded that thing, so I go out on the bridge one night and there's bunker and big fish on the bridge. This is the Meadowbrook by the way, so I walk out past the first light and there's two big fish up on top, between the first and second light. I cast that lure and I hooked the first fish right away, and he went right under the bridge. I got him out, kind of horsed him out, was pushing my luck a little, but I got him out and dragged him down to the shore, ran down the bridge and got him in.

I run back out on the bridge, my heart's pumping a hundred miles an hour, and I didn't see another fish. I was a little hesitant, you know, do I keep walking, what do I do, so I make a blind cast to the side and let it go deep. Wham, I get hammered deep, and when you get hammered deep by a big fish like that, they get away from you, and this fish took off. He got deep under the bridge and I was really putting the brakes on him, and I was worried that my line was going to snap, because he was deep. It took me a while to work him out, but I finally got him out, dragged him down and landed him. He was a big fish. When I did the math later, it came up fifty-six pounds.

So I come back out, and I'm exhausted at that point, you know what I mean [*laughs*] my heart's pumping, I walk down to the very same spot, took a couple casts, nothing, then I walked down to the next span and there was nothing on top, so I took a few sideways casts, nothing, and I'm thinking *Where are these fish?* So, I walk over to the next span and take a sideways cast, and I let it go deep and swing back under the bridge. Wham, I get smashed, that fish took off and was more than halfway under the bridge. That fish was taking drag, even with a tight drag, that fish was taking drag, I was leaning over the bridge so hard trying to pull that fish out, I think that fish took me like five or six minutes to get him out from under the bridge.

When I got him out, and I got him up top, it's amazing you know, they do that big splash, thrashing around, trying to get back down, and your pulling as hard as you can, not letting them. That's always the thing that stays etched in my memory, even when I was a kid fishing with Frank Dominic that night on the boat, and I saw that guy catch a fish from the bridge for the first time. It was dark, but I could see this big fish thrashing on the surface, off in the distance, and that really stuck in my mind. Geezzz, it's like all these years, and I'm still like a little kid. It's when I get my first look at the fish, and the fish is telling me to go f myself, and I'm telling the fish that's not going to happen. It never gets old. It's brute force, knock-down, drag out, fishing. Literally. And I love it!

And when I looked down at this fish, I knew it was a really big fish. Even from up above, I could see it was just substantially wider than the other two I had caught earlier. And I'm thinking *Wow, that's a big f'ing fish*. And when I got him down to the shore, I nosed him into the rocks, that fish stayed dead straight, hardly moved. I free-spooled it, ran down, kicked the reel in gear and flew down those rocks like a little mountain goat, got my hand on the fish's jaw and pulled him up, the fish's head was bigger than mine!

I was like *Holy Sh!t*. Like, it didn't dawn on me that the fish was in the sixties, I just knew that it was ridiculously big, much bigger than the other two I had just caught, you know. I remember, I put him in the back of my truck right away, in case a State Trooper came and kicked me off, I wasn't taking any chances with this fish. [*laughs*]

Rich: [*laughing*]

Billy: And then I went back out on the bridge, and there was a little bit of a lull. I didn't see any fish for a while.

Rich: Well, after that splash-fest, I'm not surprised [*laughs*]

Billy: Yeah! So I'm walking back and forth, and I'm half wanting to take some casts, just to see if maybe they're just hanging deep, like they were before. But I'm still so excited after catching that big fish, I wind up walking up to the third light, and there's two more fish right up on top. Right in the shadow line. I made a cast to the first one and I got him. At that point my arms were starting to get a little tired, you know. [*laughs*] I was out at the third light, and I had to drag this fish all the way into shore to land it, and when I was climbing back up the rocks, I was beginning to wonder who was beating the sh!t out of who. [*laughs*]

But I couldn't leave, you know, not yet. I went back out and there were no fish up top. I walked around looking for a while, but there was nothing. I almost gave up, I was really tired, but I was near the third light, so I started making a few sideways casts, sweeping it under the bridge, just to see if there were any fish back there. I don't remember which cast it was, but the fish hit it way back under the bridge. I was dead tired at that point, and I had a hell of a time pulling that fish out of there. But I did.

I fished for another hour, nothing, the tide was slowing, the bite was over. It was an amazing night, I was still shaking as I was driving home, and always on my mind was that world record fish. *Where the f%(k is that world record fish?* How can I be in a school of fifties and not have a record fish? It's got to be there somewhere… So anyway, I had got a couple of one hundred and eighty quart coolers from Gott, they don't make them anymore, and I kept them in my truck. One was filled with ice and bunker, and the other was filled with just ice. When I put the bass in the cooler, his head was sticking out of one side, his tail was sticking out the other, and he was almost as wide as the cooler. I couldn't close the lid. I weighed him, actually her, early the next morning, at Hudson's, and she weighed sixty-three pounds.

Rich: Four fifties and a sixty-three in one night, that's a hell of a high water mark.

Billy: I'd trade those fish for a world record in a heartbeat. You know I've fished those bridges hard for five decades looking for that fish, and the one thing that keeps me awake at night is what did I miss. I mean, I can't be on the bridge every night, and I always wonder, what did I miss? Like, I could have a couple big fish on the north side of the Meadowbrook for a couple nights, and then they were gone, and as I'm walking back over to the south side, there's like four really big fish in the line, and I'm like, *Were these fish here all the time, did I miss something, did I make a mistake?* I torture myself like that.

Rich: Here's another thing that'll really fry your brain if you think about it too much. For every one of those big fish you see up on top, in the line, there's probably two or three more down on the bottom lined up underneath.

Billy: Man, you ain't kidding! I'll tell you what, you said something to me the other night, that I have to be honest with you, I never thought about it. And when you said it, I kind of chuckled because I was like… it was when we got smoked on the Wantagh that time… me and Shawn.

Rich: Yep.

Billy: I never, ever thought about going downtide and casting under the bridge, like we normally do on that bridge. And when you said that, I was like wow, why didn't I think of that. You know, no matter how long you do this, you can always miss something. I completely missed that. I guess it was so devastating to get brutalized like that, it just didn't dawn on me at that moment. After you said that, I thought about it, I mean, could you imagine if they were downtide. We might have had a shot at getting one of those fish in!

Rich: Yep… You might have had a shot. And I'll tell you what, I'd be willing to bet my bottom dollar, that if there were enough of those fish around, and it appeared there were at the rate they were busting you up guys up, that there were probably fish on other pieces of the bridge, like the rocks.

Billy: Yeah! I mean if this was the school that the girl ran into, then they could have been in that whole span, even the next span, I don't know, we didn't get that far.

Rich: [*laughing*] You didn't get very far at all!

Billy: But you know, who knows how many of those fish were there, we were the only ones up there. That's the stuff you think about later, that keeps me awake at night. Like, when you told me that, you got my brain working, and I was like sh!t, there could have been two, three, four spans just jammed full of those giant fish!

171

Rich: And now you'll kick yourself forever for it, right?

Billy: Yeah.

Rich: It's always about the fish you didn't catch, right?

Billy: Yeah.

Rich: I should have never said anything.

Post 09/11/01…

On the morning of September 11th, 2001 the political, social, and physical landscape of this country was altered forever, when Al Qaeda terrorists hijacked four commercial passenger planes and conducted coordinated attacks on US targets. The first two planes were crashed into the Twin Towers of the World Trade Center in New York City, which subsequently collapsed. The third plane crashed into the Pentagon, and the fourth plane crashed in a field in Pennsylvania, the result of a passenger revolt. As a country, we would never be the same again.

For those readers not familiar with the area this book is based on, the nine west end bridges are located in relatively close proximity to Manhattan. At night, when we were fishing the west side of the Meadowbrook Bridge aka Big M, we could see the skyline of the city twinkling in the distance, far across the dark bay waters, and the endless jets coming and going out of JFK Airport. And on the morning of the 11th, if you lived in that vicinity, you would have no doubt seen the smoke coming from the towers as they burned.

While America had taken one hell of a shot to the throat, and was stunned and gasping for air, Manhattan, her boroughs, and the suburbs, were absolutely hemorrhaging. An estimated two thousand seven hundred people died in the Twin Towers attacks, and the devastation to Manhattan was indescribable. Beyond the grief of all the families and friends who lost loved ones, for the people who lived within this disaster's reach, there was fear, a visceral fear of vulnerability they had never felt before. And when the wind blew in your direction, it carried with it that smell.

In the immediate aftermath, nobody knew if more attacks were planned, security around all major infrastructure points was on high alert. Airports, bridges, arenas, any place where large groups of people gathered, all were being buttoned down as tight as possible. If your van stalled on the GW Bridge, or any of the major bridges in and out of the city, you could be sure that you'd be surrounded by a swat team in a matter of minutes. I remember detailed inspections of the bridge pilings being done, on not only the west end bridges, but on all the bridges of the south shore bays, and every bridge in and out of New York. Everything was being looked at closely, no stone left unturned.

I won't relate any details on how my life was impacted by the events of 9/11, other than to say that many of the people I know (and knew) were touched to varying degrees by this disaster. As the days, weeks, and months, went by, most people struggled to return to some sense of normalcy. They went to work, took their kids to soccer practice, planned the Thanksgiving holiday, all in an effort to bury the fear and sorrow that was gnawing at their soul, like cancer.

But it was also a time when people came together, where differences were put aside while everyone rolled up their sleeves, and helped dig Manhattan out of the mess left in the aftermath of the attack. Volunteers poured in from everywhere, manpower, equipment, twenty-four hours a day, it was humanity at its finest, and it went a long way in helping people cope with a disaster, the scale of which no one could have ever imagined.

Obviously, there's no subtle way for me to make the transition from something of the enormous magnitude of the 9/11 attacks, to something as insignificant as fishing from bridges, so I won't even attempt to. In its simplest form, for those of us who fished the bridges, post 9/11 brought in a new level of law enforcement that we had never seen before. It has always been illegal to fish from the bridges, but prior to 9/11, there was only token enforcement, or worst case, you pissed off a trooper by saying something stupid. Occasionally a State Trooper would come across the bridge and crank up the bull horn, "No fishing from the bridge guys" as he passed. Or one might decide to write some parking tickets because he was in a bad mood or whatever, but with few exceptions, they mostly left us alone.

But after the attacks, night time activity around important infrastructure, like bridges, was actively discouraged. Everything and everybody was considered suspicious, even some guys doing nothing more than fishing off the tops of the bridges. And the discouragement was escalated from being chased by a bull horn, to being issued summonses to appear before the court. Not only could the State Troopers issue appearance tickets, but also the Park Rangers, Bay Constables, and the DEC. And they were also towing vehicles at one point. For some time, it became an expensive proposition to fish from the top of the bridges.

For some of us, this level of enforcement brought about changes in the way we pursued our nightly business. Some of the changes you can file as obvious. The first thing that occurred to me is that I would no longer be able to just pull my vehicle off to the side of the road, past the bridge, and walk out on the bridge. My vehicle was a sitting duck for a ticket or a tow, so the first order of business was to find hiding places to park my vehicle. This became quite an involved process over the years.

The second thing I began to do was to start exploring the fishing possibilities available from the bases of the bridges, of which I discovered there were many. This kept you out of the eyes of any law enforcement driving the roads. Third, I started fishing the tops of the bridges that had walkways, this way I could duck down and hide, whenever I saw headlights coming in the distance. This actually worked pretty well, except when you had a fish on. And lastly, because I knew a good parking spot for my vehicle, at least for a time, I finally got to explore the areas around the 1st Wantagh Bridge.

On my night time drives out to the 2nd and 3rd Wantagh Bridges, I had always looked to my right as I passed over the little 1st Wantagh Bridge. The dark, narrow waters of the channel, deep in the corner of the bay, had always fascinated me, and I hadn't forgotten those paths that disappeared down the sides of bridge. Sometime in the 90s, I had discovered that there was an old abandoned electrical station just past the southwest side of the bridge. It was nothing more than a small building surrounded by a chain link fence at the bottom of the hill, accessed by a narrow asphalt driveway that dropped straight down, and then hooked right into two parking spaces, which are fully shielded from the parkway by a thick growth of trees and brush. I had driven by it many times and had never noticed it.

When I finally decided to make my first exploratory trip to the west side of the bridge, I parked down in the electrical station, hoping I hadn't outfoxed myself by trespassing on private property, and getting myself towed in the process. I made my way south across the bridge and down the path on the northwest side. The path ended on a concrete wall. To the right, the wall ran down and ended at a boulder field that descended to the shoreline and beyond. To the left, the wall angled in toward the bridge, and then to my surprise, went all the way underneath the bridge, and out the other side.

I had brought the Big Dog and a bunch of bucktails, just to get a feel for the waters. The depth of the water at the bottom of the path I had walked down appeared to be very shallow, so I opted to walk along the wall toward the bridge. When I reached the corner, where the wall turned under the bridge, I decided to test the waters and take a few casts. What I discovered in short order was that the water was deep, fast, and literally unfishable. Apparently, after the last rebuild of that bridge, all the scrape concrete and rebar had been dumped on the bottom creating an unforgiving sticky mass of structure. It was the most hopeless stretch of bottom I had ever experienced. You couldn't even feel trouble coming. I decided to move on to greener pastures.

Under normal circumstances, that would have been the end of it, there seemed little point in beating that dead horse, and I couldn't help but think of the age old adage that "you don't leave fish to find fish". Despite the appealing look of those waters, I probably would have never given that area another look. But roll the clock ahead to a night in late April of 2003, and once again, as luck and happenstance would have it, I found myself in Nassau County, heading home after an evening out with friends. I decided to take the quiet route and exited southbound on to the Wantagh Parkway, figuring it would be nice to ride over the bridges after the long winter. Just past the 1st Wantagh Bridge, I hit the brakes hard, making the impulsive decision to pull down into the old electrical station. It was quite the fancy maneuver. After sitting around yapping it up with friends all night, and the long winter, I really craved some salt air.

After killing the lights, I got out and made my way up the entrance ramp and over toward the bridge. That's when I first heard it. There was literally no wind, I'm talking dead calm, you could have heard a pin drop, but that was not what I was hearing. I ran across the bridge and stumbled down the path, and when I got to the bottom and looked out onto the bay, I could not believe what I was saw! There were bass feeding everywhere! There had to hundreds of them, feeding on the surface! The water's surface was like glass, except for the current, and there was plenty of ambient light, so you could see everything. And the noise, the noise was extraordinary! There was so much feeding noise, I could hardly hear myself think. I was stunned.

I looked down into the shallow water around the base of the wall where I stood and I could see the fins of bass cruising through the water in all directions. They seemed to be everywhere, except under the bridge, or the main channel where the wall cut under the bridge, the very same deep, snaggy area that I casted to years before, and had given the bridge a thumbs down on. I turned right and walked down to where the wall ended and scrambled down the rocks to the shoreline. I followed it out about sixty yards or so, to a sod bank point where the water opened to the right, leading into a channel that lead back to a marina. I stood on the point and looked out upon that mass of feeding fish, trying to process what I was witnessing, and had absolutely no point of reference from which to draw.

Looking directly west, across the channel that leads into the marina, lies Oliver's Island, and all around the island was a mass of striped bass feeding. Whatever they were feeding on was being flushed out of the marina channel also. Ocean blitzes are not an uncommon occurrence, most fishermen who have been around a while have seen them, but I have never witnessed this kind of feeding mayhem, on such a large scale, in the bay, at night, before. And the fish didn't move, they just stayed put and grinded through the tide.

Speaking of the tide, at some point my stunned senses starting giving way to my need to know, observational nature. I looked at the current and quickly realized that the tide was outgoing. I looked on the sod bank and found the wet eel grass, high tide mark, looked at the rocks, the tide line on the wall, etc. and figured the tide had been dropping for a while. I stuck my hand in the water to see how warm it was, and it felt pretty warm for late April. The quarter moon was easy enough considering there wasn't a cloud in the sky.

The only thing I couldn't see was the bait. My guess is that it was probably grass shrimp, but that's only because I know the bait patterns of that area now. But whatever it was, there was a ton of it, and it kept those fish on the feed the entire time I was there, which was for about another hour. It was hard for me to leave, but when I finally did, I left with an epiphany, and a whole lot to think about. What I had inadvertently stumbled upon was an early season bite of epic proportions, that I never knew existed. It would serve as my spring wake up call for many years, until Hurricane Sandy flushed out the bay and wiped out the food chain.

The 2nd Wantagh Bridge had two things that made it immediately appealing during the post 9/11 crackdown around the bridges. The first was an old stretch of dirt parking road behind a stand of trees and brush just past the northeast side of the bridge. As soon as you cross the bridge heading north, you pull over past the guard railing onto the bicycle path, and then turn sharply right down a dirt hill, and then make a sharp left onto the dirt road. The other end of the dirt road exited back up onto the bicycle path about fifty yards down. It was considered curtesy among bridge fishermen to pull forward far enough, to allow at least one other vehicle to pull in behind you. In our little world of bridge fishing, this was the cat and mouse reality that was being ushered in post 9/11.

The second thing that made fishing this bridge desirable was that it had the concrete dividers between the roadway and the walkway from which we fished. You can't see through concrete. You could also see headlights coming from a long distance off, in both directions, long before anybody in a vehicle could see you. During the fall when we were fishing the bridges, there wasn't much traffic on these roads, so this gave you plenty of time to take evasive action. This usually entailed reeling in your jig, and laying down on the sidewalk until the offending vehicle passed by. If you had a fish on, then you would lean your rod against the railing and hold the butt while lying down on the ground, and hope that nobody noticed the bent and bobbing rod. It worked most of the time.

The 2nd Wantagh Bridge had the high chain link fence on the east side, and one of the hot spots we used to fish from on the bridge stands, was the second span on the southeast side. There is a very sticky ridge that comes up around three feet off the bottom, right about at the shadow line, that the bass would line up on. Sometimes there were so many bass there, I figured they must be three deep, across the whole span. At some point, I started wondering if I could reach that ridge from somewhere down around the base of the bridge, and still be able to pull fish out of there to land them. It would be great if I could, because fishing down below removed me from the view of the law driving the roads. I had fished some of the other, kinder, bridges from base locations, but none of them were nearly as gnarly as the 2nd Wantagh. It was a long shot, but nothing ventured, nothing gained.

In many regards, fishing is basically nothing more than problem solving, at least that's the way I've always looked at it. If I was going to figure out a way to pull bass off of that ridge at the second span, from a shore bound location, then I was going to have to science the sh!t out of it. The first thing I needed to determine was the optimum place to cast from. It couldn't be too near the bridge base because I would have no angle what so ever in which to pull fish out. Every cast would just drift into the ridge, so fishing anywhere parallel to the bridge was dismissed immediately. It had to be further away from the base, so I started moving out away from the bridge, following the rocks along the shore, until I found what I was looking for. It was a chunk of concrete slab laying relatively flat, right at the water's edge. It made a perfect casting platform, about thirty yards away from the base of the bridge. First problem solved.

Based on the distance and location of my casting platform to the distance of the second span, this gave me about a thirty-degree angle to the face of the bridge. It was not a lot, but it was doable if I struck hard and fast. The next problem was getting the bucktail over the three foot ridge. For this problem I was actually well equipped already, and a quick explanation of hydrodynamics will explain why. The water at the 2nd Wantagh is deep, twenty something feet, with very strong current. Those of us who fish the bridges use fifty pound test monofilament line almost exclusively on our reels, for a lot of reasons. And it just so happens that fifty pound mono has a large diameter and is fairly light, which means it offers a lot of resistance to water. This can be both a blessing and a curse depending on what you want your line to do. In this case, it was both.

After experimenting with a few different weight bucktails and casting angles I finally came up with a formula. From the position on my casting platform, in order for my bucktail to enter the strike zone, I had to bomb a cast straight out ninety degrees from shore, basically thirty yards parallel to the shadow line of the bridge, and just past the end of the second span, engage the reel, and then wait for the bucktail to touch down. I eventually determined an expected count down before touch down, to keep me on my toes. The thick diameter line slowed the bucktails descent to the bottom, but if I had landed the bucktail where I wanted to, it would touch down about ten feet or so in front of the shadow line and slightly past the ridge.

At that point, I would lift my rod tip sharply and start reeling like mad. This is where hydrodynamics comes in to play. What would happen is the pressure of the moving water against the thick fifty-pound mono line would lift the bucktail right off the bottom and float it right up, across, and over the ridge, pretty as pie, and right into the maw of a hungry bass, a maneuver not possible with thinner, braided line. Then the real fun would begin.

The very first double tap hit I got off that ridge sent a bolt of adrenalin through my veins. I hit back hard and immediately took a step back and started short pumps and leans with all my strength. I quickly learned that you had to get the jump on them, and if you did, then they would all move to the left, and they wouldn't be able to make it to the piling if you locked down on them. After that, they would usually move out into the tide, but if you got lazy for a second, they would turn on you and bolt for the bridge. It was intense fun, but for full disclosure, I definitely got smoked more than once by good fish. I also discovered that the water under the concrete slab I casted and landed fish from, was a bit undercut and fairly deep, as the bass would scoot around under there, fraying my line on some of the rocks down there. Checking the first eight feet of line and retying the bucktail after every fish became standard procedure in quick order, and ignoring standard procedure had consequences, as I learned a couple years on.

On that particular night, I had been chased from the top of the 2nd and had driven to the D&D for a cup of coffee. There were a ton of fish on the bridge that night, so I wasn't giving up that easy. I finished my coffee and headed back southbound on the Wantagh Parkway. About a quarter mile before the 2nd Wantagh Bridge, there is a sharp turn off onto a little dirt road that goes back a little ways. If you blink, you miss it. It was probably created by the duck hunters in the area, but all I cared about was that my vehicle could not be spotted from the road when I parked all the way in the back. I killed my lights early, turned in, and drove to the back. I got out, worked my way against the brush to the back of my Blazer, hoping I didn't pick up a bunch a ticks along the way, grabbed the Big Dog, and headed out to the road.

The parkway was empty. I quickly crossed to the bicycle path side and began my trek up to the bridge. No vehicles came either way the whole trip to the bridge, which was good because I didn't feel like running down the hill and hiding in the tick infested brush. When I got to the bridge, I quickly crossed to the south side and made my way down the rocks, and worked my way along the shore, out to my casting rock. I was winded and needed a short rest before fishing, so I just sat for a few minutes taking in the silhouette of the bridge against the night sky, the sound of the water, and the thick smell of salt. I don't know why, but the 2nd Wantagh with that bridge operator's tower made of stone, sitting out in the middle of the bay, always seemed kind of spooky to me late at night, when nobody was around for miles. Anyway, I remember the conditions being very moderate, somewhere between a moon, so the current wasn't pushing like crazy, and there was just enough breeze to keep the mosquitos at bay, at least most of time. It was a good night to fish.

185

I unhooked the two and a half ounce Andrus bucktail with a #70 Uncle Josh pork rind trailer from my rod, took aim, and bombed my first cast. It landed right on target, so I began my countdown to the bottom. It touched down right on time, so I lifted the rod tip and started cranking and got the bucktail right over and across the ridge. It was hit immediately and it was game on. It was a smaller fish, mid-teen size, and I dragged it in as fast as I could, yanked it up, popped the bucktail out of its jaw and dumped it back, fins up. I didn't feel any rubbing of the line on the rocks below me, so I didn't bother checking my line. I was amped up now, so I immediately fired off another cast.

Another perfect landing, resulting in another hook up, this time a much better fish. Now I was having fun! I leaned on this fish to death to get her in and eventually got her close and running back and forth under my feet. I reeled down on her, locked up the reel with my fingers, and practically snapped the Big Dog in half dragging her up. As soon as her head popped up, I wrapped the line around my arm a couple times and hauled her up on the rock. She was better than the first, fat, in the upper twenties. I unhooked her, and slide her right off the rock back into the water, and she took off. I took a short, cursory feel of the line ahead of the bucktail, didn't feel anything and figured I was good, so I reeled in the rest of the line and prepared for another cast. I was on fire.

Fast forward to the hook up, another good fish. I did what I always do. I took a step back, raised my rod as high as it would go, and leaned back with all my weight. The folly of this tactic is that it relies on the equal power of the fish pulling against you to hold you up. No fish, nothing to hold you up, so when the line snapped, I pitched straight back, no hope of recovery, without a clue of what was behind me. I was fortunate. Instead of a jagged granite rock, the kind that was literally everywhere down there, the back of my head made contact with the edge of a chuck of flat concrete slab, not unlike the kind I was casting from. Out went the lights.

When I finally started to come around and open my eyes, the first thing they saw was a rat sniffing my right hand. I didn't understand what I was seeing at first, but when it finally registered with my brain, I sat straight up. That's when the bolt of pain shot through my skull. Everything went black and white and sparkly and I almost passed out again. I thought I was going to puke. Fortunately the rat took off into the rocks. I had no idea of how long I was out; I've never worn a watch. As I sat there, I felt behind my head and could feel some tacky blood on my Rangers cap, so I guess I cracked my noggin pretty hard.

I slowly got to my feet, using the Big Dog for support, but I was pretty woozy. I reeled in my line and made my way very slowly along the shore, and then basically crawled up the rocks for fear of falling again. Once up top, I started the interminable walk back to my truck, a quarter mile down the road, shaky, nauseous, and head pounding all the way. I barely remember the ride home. I should have gone to the hospital as I no doubt had a concussion. I didn't. To quote Forrest Gump, "Stupid is as stupid does." I suppose I could have died in my sleep that night, and I wasn't right for weeks.

Rich: Yeah, things got pretty dicey after 9/11. I'm guessing you took more than your fair share of abuse fishing the up front bridges.

Billy: You bet I did! There was a lot more traffic on the Meadowbrook and the Loop because that was one of the main ways out to Point Lookout and Lido Beach, so I was constantly hitting the deck when cars would come over the bridge. But if I had a fish, there wasn't much I could do, I was a sitting duck. You know the State Troopers didn't really bother us much before 9/11. I mean they'd chase us off sometimes and give us a parking ticket once in a while. But right after 9/11 they got serious, and a couple got downright mean. Things got pretty crazy, and sometimes a little scary.

Rich: Yeah, they sure did.

Billy: There was this one trooper, you know who I'm talking about, this guy was nuts, and he hated me because I was always on the bridges. We all knew him because he called the bridges, "his bridges". Like, he would stop his cruiser right in the middle of the parkway and get out and start yelling, "If you mother fu$k#rs aren't off my bridge in thirty seconds I'm going to arrest you all and impound your vehicles!" I mean this guy was just plain crazy. Funny thing though, he didn't really give out tickets, and I mean

188

appearance tickets for fishing on the bridge, where you had to go to court, you know. Other State Troopers were handing them out left and right, but this guy didn't, he was just mean and nasty, and did some crazy sh!t.

Listen to this. One night he comes over the Meadowbrook and there's like three of us fishing. He spots us and stops in the middle of the parkway, and hops out of his cruiser. He goes into his rant and he climbs over the railing and comes onto the walkway. I'm wondering what the f is he up to now. Two of the guys had caught fish that they were keeping and they were laying on the walkway. This guy is screaming at us, and he comes up to the first guy and kicks his fish off the bridge into the water, a dead fish, just kicks it in the water, while screaming in this guy's face. Then he does the same to the other guy's fish. I don't think those guys had ever come across this trooper before, because they literally ran off the bridge, and I can't recall ever seeing them again [*laughs*]

Rich: [*laughing*]

Billy: By the time he got to me, I thought he was going to stroke out. I just started walking down toward my truck. He got back in his cruiser and followed me in the right lane, yelling at me on the bull horn all the way. I mean this guy was bat sh!t crazy, you know… he had no business having a badge. Then, me and Jeff were on the 3rd Wantagh one night, really late. There had been bunker under the lights and bass on the bunker, so the few other guys there had been snagging the bunker and then leaving them on the street. The tide died, those guys left and it was just me and Jeff. It was like 4:30 a.m. so Jeff and I decided to kick the dead bunker into the water so the gulls wouldn't be eating them, and cars wouldn't be hitting the gulls, and we wouldn't catch sh!t for leaving the dead bunker on the road.

So, Jeff's on the north side of the bridge and I'm working the south side of the bridge, when you know who comes flying over the bridge, and comes to a screeching halt in front of me. I mean he almost hit me, I actually jumped back. I was surprised to see him because it was way past his shift. He jumps out of his cruiser and goes straight into his usual yelling about fishing on his bridges. At that point I was really tired, and I just wanted to go home, and I really wasn't in the mood for his sh!t. I had leaned my rod against the rail, about twenty feet down. He sees it and goes over, picks it up and holds it over the rail, like he's going to drop it in the water. I said, "Don't even think about it!"

He comes racing over with the rod and yells, "What did you say?" I said, "Don't even think about it!" He slams the rod down, pulls out his hand cuffs and cuffs me to the railing! First time in my life I got a little nervous with this guy, I mean, I didn't know if this nut was going to shoot me or what, I'm thinking this guy is f'ing crazy, you know. [*laughing*]

Rich: [*laughing*] Wow.

Billy: So listen, he gave me the full lecture on the bridge, like you can't do this anymore. But he was a strange dude, he hated me, and he yelled at me all the time, but he never gave me a ticket, never gave me a ticket… So he uncuffs me and goes, "I don't want to see you up here again! If I do, I'm going to arrest you and impound your truck!" Same sh!t that he always says, and he left! Completely nuts! And you remember this. I was in Dunkin' Donuts one night, it's like 4:30 a.m. and I'm done fishing, and he walks in. He starts yelling at me in Dunkin' Donuts, and I'm not even fishing! [*laughing*] So I say, "Look, I was fishing these bridges long before you were a cop, and I'll still be fishing them when you're no longer a cop." As I got up to leave I thought I saw steam coming out of his ears [*laughing*]

Rich: [*laughing*] I bet he was on the hunt for you the next night!

Billy: Actually, I took about a week off, I still wasn't convinced that he wasn't crazy enough to snap and shoot me, I mean he was really crazy, you know. The only good thing I think he ever did was help Jeff one night when he caught Shawn and Jeff fishing from the scaffolds on the 2nd. He came back there yelling and screaming while Shawn was helping Jeff land a mid-twenty pound bass, and Shawn dropped the bass and took off and the gaff went right through Jeff's hand. So he's yelling at Jeff until he saw the blood pouring out of Jeff's hand and Jeff struggling with this fish, so he stopped his yelling and

191

helped him. I was a little pissed at Shawn for taking off like that, but that's another story for another day.

Rich: Well, I pretty much avoided him over on the Wantaghs. I got bull horned off the 3rd several times with the usual threats of vehicle impoundments and whatnot, but I kept a fairly low profile, literally, over there. He took me and my friend by surprise one night at the 2nd. I was parked pretty deep down in the dirt road, so he must have parked up on the parkway and walked down. We had leaned our rods against an old sign down there and were loading our fish in the back of my Blazer, so our backs were to him. All of a sudden he lights us up with his flashlight and starts yelling about us trespassing and how he's going to impound my vehicle. Scared the crap out of me and my friend. He goes on for a few minutes then tells us to get the f out of there before he decides to arrest us. We jumped in my Blazer and blew out the other end of the dirt road and up onto the parkway headed north.

Billy: Yeah, that was definitely him [*laughing*]

Rich: We got about a mile down the parkway before we realized we had left our rods leaning on the sign.

Billy: Oh sh!t [*laughing*]

Rich: So now we're like, we got to go back and get them, but if that asshole sees my Blazer, I'm screwed. So I went all the way down to Merrick Road, came back up south to the circle at Jones, and then headed back down the parkway to the 2nd. Didn't see another car the whole time, man my butthole was clinched tighter than a clam. [*laughing*] As I crossed over the 2nd, I killed the lights and pulled over, and my friend shot out of the passenger seat, ran down and grabbed the rods, ran back up and put them up in the rod holders, and we bolted out of there. Needless to say, that parking spot was blown.

Billy: Yeah, there was a lot of cat and mouse stuff with the parking. You could write a book on all the parking spots we came up with during the decades we fished the bridges. We'd make'em, they'd find'em and close them off.

Rich: You got that right. Making parking spaces was my favorite winter hobby, [*laughing*] I even made a drop down ghillie suit for the back of my Blazer. [*laughs*]

Billy: [*laughing*]

Rich: But the fishing was so good at that point, I mean insanely good, the bridges were just loaded with fish. You just couldn't stay away.

Billy: You ain't lying. I was out with Jeff one night, and there were big fish on the bridge. I had just caught a good fish, an upper forty, but there were bigger fish there, and I had landed it and we were standing at the back of my truck. A trooper pulls up, starts giving us the you can't fish here speech, and he gives us the third degree, and

193

Jeff gets a little scared… well I shouldn't say scared, that's probably not the right word, Jeff was always very law abiding, you know what I mean?

Rich: Yup.

Billy: So, we had parked his truck at Causeway, and we had gone in mine, you know. So I drive all the way back, and he goes, "What are you going to do?" I said, "I'm going right back, what are you kidding me, there's big fish all over the bridge." So he goes, "Your kidding?" I go, "No, I'm going back." So I dropped him off because he said he didn't want to take the chance. I said, "OK, goodbye." And I went back. I didn't get on that bridge two minutes, and this f'ing trooper shows up. He must have been following me, or whatever, and he goes, "You got to be stupid or something!" and I hate when they say that to me, because it's not like I'm stupid asshole, there's big fish here! So, he kicks me off… he didn't give me a ticket, but this asshole follows me all the way to Merrick Road, until I got off the freaking parkway. So I went down to the D&D and had a cup of coffee. I was going to go back out again, but then I figured three times was pushing it. Man, it was hard to leave those fish, you know.

Merry Christmas!

Billy: Right after 9/11 law enforcement on the bridges became a problem, I mean, they really started coming down hard on us fishermen. Instead of an occasional parking ticket, they started handing out a steady stream of summonses, which sucked, because they required a court appearance. I racked up five in no time and the day I was scheduled to go to court, it was like a week before Christmas. So I show up at court, and my name gets called, and I go before the judge, and he looks down at the case, and he goes, "Let's see now... Mr. Legakis, you have four, make that five summonses for fishing from a bridge, where it is clearly posted that no fishing is allowed." And I said, "Yes Your Honor." Then he looks down at me and says, "And you understood that you weren't supposed to be fishing from the bridge, is that correct?" And I said, "Yes Your Honor."

He looks directly at me for a couple seconds and says, "You don't look stupid, so why would you keep doing something if you knew you were going to get more summonses?" He shuffled through the summonses, "These are dated a day apart, why is that?" I reached into my pocket and pulled out five pictures I had brought with me, and handed them up to him. The pictures were of four fifties and a sixty. He took them and looked at them, then he looks at me over his glasses and goes, "You caught these from the bridge?" I said, "Yes Your Honor." He hands them back to me and looks at the court recorder person and says, "I think the court will give Mr. Legakis here a little early Christmas present and dismiss his summonses. Mr. Legakis, you are free to go.

Rich: Yeah, I know exactly what you mean. The Wantaghs were as packed as I've ever seen them, and even though we were starting to get the troopers timing down, it was still tough when you were hooking up on every cast, only to get bull horned off the bridge, or get ticketed. County cops don't patrol the parkways, but there was a County cop who was a fisherman, and he used to stop by all the time and watch us fish. He was a cool dude. One night I was on the 2nd doing the usual duck and wait thing, and I hooked a good fish on the downtide side, by the second light on the south side. The fish had me off the bridge a ways when headlights were coming up fast southbound.

Billy: Trooper?

Rich: That's what I figured. There was no way I was walking this fish down in time, so I moved to the left of the light a bit, leaned the rod against the rail, hit the deck, and waited. The car came up quick and then stopped. I didn't see any flashers go on, but I heard the door open and shut and the sound of somebody walking toward me, and then stop. I figured I was toast, so I looked up. Against the street light, all I could see was the outline of an official looking figure, with an official looking hat, bending over the traffic divider looking at me. Then he spoke. He said, "Don't you think you should reel your fish in."

Billy: [*laughing*]

196

Rich: It was that Nassau County cop, he spotted the rod, he knew we did this stuff, so he spotted it right away. [*laughing*] As I got up, I told him he almost made me sh!t my pants. He started laughing, put his flashers on and stuck around long enough to watch me land the fish, then took off. I got some funny County cop stories. I was headed to fish the 1st Wantagh late one night in the spring and as I crossed over the bridge I killed my lights in preparation for pulling down into the old power station. So I go flying down the entrance and as I'm making the hard right into the parking space, I see a County cop, backed into the far space, cab light on, magazine open on the wheel, and he's slapping little Johnny behind the ear!

Billy: Oh sh!t [*laughing*]

He sees my dark blue Blazer appear out of thin air and out goes the cab light, and I guess he scrambled around to get himself ship shape. I pulled in right next to him and pretended I didn't see a thing. I just hop out of my Blazer, go to the back, drop the tailgate, and start putting on my waders. He eventually comes out of his cruiser and comes over. He's a young guy, and asks me what I'm doing. I said, "I'm going fishing." He asks me if I park here often and I tell him I do. He then asks me if the State Troopers have a problem with me parking here and I say, "No." I guess that was enough for him, so he gets in his cruiser and leaves.

Billy: That could have been a sticky situation [*laughs*]

197

Rich: [*laughing*] Geezzz, Never thought about that! Then one night I was walking out from the Wantagh Park Marina to the 1st, the clam bar, you know where I'm talking about.

Billy: Yeah. Where you almost got ran down by that cabin cruiser.

Rich: Yup, but that's a whole other story for another time… Anyway, I'm walking along, bicycle paths everywhere, and it's a long walk, All the way in the back, at the farthest point where the park ends, there's a large bicycle circle around a fountain or statue, and as I approach this, I see something parked there. As I get closer, I realize it's a Nassau County Police car, lights out, both inside and out, and I'm wondering what fresh hell is this? Right about that time, I must have come into view of the occupant(s), because that cruiser took off at light speed on the opposite path from mine, no lights, I'm guessing so I couldn't read the plates. I suspect the cop inside was probably getting a hand job from some bimbo and thought he had found a safe place to get it. Boy, did he take off. [*laughing*]

Billy: [*laughing*]

Rich: So Billy, how long do you think the grip lasted for. I figure they started letting up after a year, maybe a year and a half. What do you think?

Billy: Yeah, I would agree with that, somewhere around a year and a half. I think a lot of them got tired of ticketing the same old guys, when they knew we posed no threat. We just wanted to fish, you know. They could still be a pain in the ass sometimes, like the Bay Constable, he was an asshole, but you just had to fish around his shift. But it did ease up over time, which was good, because the fishing was really good. I mean the bay was just loaded with fish, and some really big fish too. Listen to this, I know you hated the Swift, but I had this one night on the Swift, it was late, after everybody's shift. I was headed east on the Loop and I looked in my rearview mirror, you could see for miles because it was just a straight run, you know, and nobody was on the road.

I came up to the Swift Creek Bridge and stopped my truck on the parkway. I hopped out and ran around my truck and looked into the shadow line, and there were two giant fish just sitting next to each other, noses right up on the line. Now, you know the Swift is like the lowest bridge of all the bridges, so you can see the fish real good in the shadow line, and these were really big fish. I was like, holy crap, look at that, so I ran back to my truck and took off to the exit for the Meadowbrook, flew over the bridge, got turned around at the clover leaf at Jones, flew back over the Meadowbrook Bridge, got back on the Loop and jumped off before the Swift into the parking spot. That really killed a lot of time, and I was hoping those fish would still be there.

I grabbed my rod and ran across the parkway and looked into the shadow line and sure enough those fish were gone! I was so f'ing mad. But I figured they were still in the area and had probably dropped down to the bottom, so I decided to start bouncing bottom for them. Now all I had on my rod was my special one and a quarter ounce bullet head jig, with the 8/0 hooks I made. They have a ton of bucktail tied to them, and I fish them with a cut down two inch strip of red and white pork rind on the hook. They're made to float into the shadow line, not for bottom bouncing, so casting them far enough to get them down, with fifty pound mono, without throwing a bird's nest, was not so easy. [*laughs*]

Rich: I bet. I used to hook my bucktail to the rail, walk backwards, and let out thirty yards of line, and then engage the reel and stretch the hell out of the line to take the coil memory out of it. Helped cut down the over spooling on the back casts.

Billy: That's a good idea… So anyway, I remembered where these fish were, I figured they probably just submarined on me, so I casted my bucktail straight out as far as I could get it, and let it sink. On the second cast I got hit right as the bucktail bounced into the shadow line. That fish turned and blew straight under the bridge, I mean I didn't even have a chance to blink. My rod smacked the bridge that fish was moving so fast, and was deep. Big fish on the Swift fight different than they do on the Meadowbrook. The Swift doesn't have much current. On the Meadowbrook, when you lock those fish down, the current tends to bring those fish up right away, or they move up into the tide. They don't like the current pushing on them.

But on the Swift, they don't have a lot of current pushing on them, so they go deep, and they stay down, and they don't move. Sometimes I almost think I've hooked a big ray or something, they're that stubborn, you know… So this fish has my rod pinned against the bridge and I can't really get him to move much. He's moving around the third span and I'm pulling, and I gain some line and he takes it back, and it goes on like this for a little while, but eventually he starts moving out from under the bridge, but he's still on the bottom. So I run down to the end of the bridge and start working my way down to where I can land him, which on the Swift is actually quite a distance from the base of the bridge.

Now I'm fighting this fish from the shore, out in the open, away from the bridge, and he still hasn't come up yet. And I'm thinking, sh!t this is a strong f'ing fish, you know, he's really having his way with me. I had to be very patient. Finally, he gave up the ghost and I got him in. That fish had enormous girth, I mean really wide, it was a really strong fish. I dragged it up the side of the bridge and over to my truck and got it packed away, then I tried a few casts for the other fish, but figured that was it for the night. It was fifty-six pounds when I weighed it the next morning. That was one tough fish.

Rich: That's a nice fish.

201

Billy: Yeah, but I really would have liked to have caught that other one, you know.

Rich: Yeah, it's always about the fish you didn't catch right? [laughs]

Billy: Yeah… So the following night, Jeff and I are driving past the Swift in Jeff's truck. I tell Jeff to hit the brakes and I jump out, go to rail and do a quick scan. A little ways down there's a big fish sitting right up in the shadow line. Our rods are sticking out of the center back window of Jeff's pickup truck, and I wanted to grab my rod, but I didn't have enough time because there was a car bearing down on us at like 60 miles an hour, so I jumped back in and told Jeff to hit it. We went through the whole drive over the Meadowbrook thing to get back to the Swift so we could park, but by then, the fish was gone. I was pissed. I wanted to stay and fish the bridge for a bit, but it was late and Jeff wanted to leave, and it was his truck, so we left. I wasn't too happy about that.

The next night was a new moon, so I figured that big fish might still be hanging around the Swift, and maybe might have a few friends with him, so I decided to go out by myself. It was a late tide. I got off the ramp for the Loop Parkway and was just starting to back my truck up into the dirt road, when a vehicle with one of those spot lights mounted on the top of the cab, comes roaring up in front of me, and lights me up. I mean this light is right in my face, blinding me. Now I don't even know who this guy is, I'm assuming he's a cop of some kind, but I don't know anything for sure. So he gets out, and I see him draw his gun.

Rich: Oh sh!t!

Billy: And he goes, "Don't move!" Now, I'm in the van, I'm sitting in the seat, and I'm not moving. He goes, "Get out of the van s-l-o-w-l-y!" I get out the van, it's like three o'clock in the morning, I'm all by myself, there's no one in sight… and I'm a little leery of what's going on, you know. I mean, this guy might not be a cop for all I know, you know what I mean. So I'm wearing my standard painter's pants, blue one-piece pullover, no zipper, with the hood down, and I got a spare spool, a bunch of bucktails and pork rind in the pouch, right. So I get out of the van, and he's got the spotlight right on me, so he goes, "What's in your pocket?" I was like, "Spool, bucktails, pork rind." He goes, "What are you doing out here?" I said, "I'm fishing." He goes, "Are you right handed or left handed!" I said, "I'm right handed." He goes, "Put your right hand on your head and empty what's in your pocket out s-l-o-w-l-y!" And this guy's leaning over his fender with the gun pointed straight at me! It was getting a little nerve wracking for a moment, you know what I mean.

Rich: Sh!t yeah, I'd be browning my shorts! [*laughs*]

Billy: I'm like f&(k, I'm not one hundred percent sure what's going on here, I'm a little nervous, this f'ing idiot

203

could shoot me and no one would be the wiser. I take the stuff out of my pocket and throw it all on the ground, and he comes over, looks at it, and then then he looks at me and he goes, "What's in the van!" I said, "Painting equipment." He says, "Open it!" So I open it and he looks and he goes, "All right, listen you're not allowed to fish up here. We're looking for some poachers, and I thought you might have been one of them, now get out of here!" Boy, I'll tell you what, three o'clock in the morning, out all by yourself, with a guy pointing a gun at you, and a spotlight in your face, that can be a little nerve wracking.

Rich: I bet... So after that guy left, did you circle back and go after that fish? [*laughing*]

Billy: [*laughing*]

Despite the problems with law enforcement, the financial costs incurred, and the cat and mouse games that ensued, we had to fish, because the fishing was just getting better and better and better. Each spring, the bass were pouring into the bay in prodigious numbers, first the smaller fish in April, but quickly followed by the bigger fish in May. By mid-May, the bridges were usually stacked and come June, some really big fish would make their presence known. There were so many bass on the bridges that I would accidentally snag them. And in the fall, it would happen all over again.

We were hitting the peak of the striped bass recovery and the uniqueness of the bay's bait patterns, and the structure of the bridges combined to provide everything the bass needed to hold them there, spring and fall. They became the very definition of "resident fish", and it was impossible for us to stay away. I can't even fathom what the bottoms of these bridges must have looked like when they were loaded up with bass, there were just so many of them. And as the pressure of legal enforcement began to ease off over time, the sheer quantity of fish just drove the addiction that much harder. It was damn the torpedoes, full speed ahead!

Back in the days when we were young, had energy to burn, and the fish were stacked like cord wood.

Goodbye To The 3rd Wantagh Bridge…

I doubt that any of us who fished the bridges back then can remember the exact date when they first heard that the 3rd Wantagh Bridge was going to be torn down and rebuilt from the bottom up. The rumors started circulating sometime in the early 2000's. When the news finally reached my ears, a darkness descended upon my fishing soul. I know this will sound completely corny, but I felt a very strong attachment to that particular bridge. I had put so much work into learning the intricacies of it, that I hated the idea that all that hard work, and knowledge, would be lost. That bridge was a bitch, plain and simple, but I had made it *my* bitch, and I was angry that she was going to be taken from me.

I watched with a mixture of fascination and horror as they built the temporary bridge that ran parallel to the 3rd on its east side. It looked like some engineer on acid, who played with Erector Sets as a kid designed it. I didn't think it would last a year before it collapsed due to the powerful current that ran through the channel. By five or six years in, when I would be down underneath it fishing, you could actually see it move when cars went over it. I avoided crossing over it unless it was absolutely necessary.

I continued to fish the 3rd Wantagh proper, right up to the bitter end. Cars were already crossing over the new temporary bridge, barges were anchored nearby, cranes and other construction equipment were on site, I knew it was close. And then it happened, the lights went out on the 3rd Wantagh Bridge for the final time. It was the end of an era, and a part of my bridge fishing enthusiasm went dark with the lights. The barge moved right in after and took a couple of the center spans out. Some of the regulars, walked out and fished the part of the bridge that still stood, in the dark. I couldn't bring myself to do that. It seemed wrong to me, like I would be feeding off a wounded animal or something, it just seemed, I don't know, disrespectful.

While Billy continued his pursuit of a world record fish on the up front bridges, I started fishing the 2nd Wantagh Bridge regularly because I couldn't stand to watch the carnage going on at the 3rd. As if having sympathy on me, the 2nd treated me to some really good fishing, including some of the biggest fish I had caught from those bridges, including my personal best at the time, a forty-six pound fish. The 2nd started getting crowded as the 3rd was completely disassembled, so I started moving around to some of the other bridges up front, mostly the Meadowbrook. I felt un-homed and adrift, and it was at that point that I started to expand my range by exploring the bay areas around the bridges. As I pushed deeper into the bays, where no other fishermen went, I became amazed at what I discovered. But that is another story for another book.

Out of the nine west end bridges, the three Wantagh bridges are unique for several reasons. First off, they are the deepest bridges in the bay, meaning they are furthest from Jones Inlet. The 1st Wantagh Bridge, which is actually named the Flat Creek Bridge, and is the deepest of all the nine west end bridges, was notable for its massive early season bass bite. The 2nd and 3rd Wantagh Bridges were unique because they were the only bridges of the nine that had bottom structure, with the 3rd having the most bottom structure by far. It was the bottom structure that created the artificial reefs, and subsequent ecosystem that supported the food chain, that held the resident bass population. No other bridge held anywhere near the number of striped bass that the 3rd Wantagh Bridge did. The 3rd Wantagh Bridge died, but the memories live on.

Rich: By the time I started fishing the Wantagh bridges, the loop cast back under the bridge was already the established way of fishing those bridges. I never used it on any of the other bridges, it doesn't work, but I never really heard about how it got started on the Wantaghs.

Billy: Well… for quite a while we fished the uptide side of the 3rd from the bridge stands, I even cut the fence at one point and rolled it back, and that was easy to fish from but it was hard to land the fish from there, you know. So none of that stuff worked very well and I had had enough of working my ass off to catch fish, so I said, you know what, I got to try the other side. I really didn't take it that serious at first, because I was just frustrated with fishing from the top of the fence, with your line rubbing on the bridge and you breaking big fish off.

So… I started playing around downtide, and it took a little while to get used to, a couple days to really, like, feel the bottom, start to figure it out, and of course, get snagged a couple times. And then I figured it out, and boy, it was a whole different world! And we just stayed on the downtide side. It was the only bridge that consistently produced fish downtide. And that bridge held numbers like I've never seen on any other bridge, and by the time you came and started to learn that, the late 80s and all through the 90s, there was a huge body of fish that showed up on that bridge, you know.

But most of the guys, they really weren't good at it, it was very hard to get the right feel because you got a real strong current, and we would cast under the bridge, almost like surf casting for Chri'sake. We'd whip that bucktail thirty yards under that bridge as hard as we could, and sometimes pull out extra line, just to reach the bottom, and the line would precede the bucktail.

Rich: Yeah, that was down on the north side, just past the middle of the bridge, what was it, like thirty-six feet, or something like that.

Billy: Forty feet… yeah, so a lot of those guys wouldn't realize that their bucktail had hit the bottom, and they'd be watching their line go out, and by the time they realized they had already hit bottom, they were snagged. That's why ninety percent of the guys who came to fish that bridge gave up on it. They'd lose bucktail after bucktail, and back then bucktails weren't cheap, they were like three bucks a pop, and that was a lot of money back then. I remember Little Teddy lost like six bucktails in an hour, he was like, "I'm done with this!" He hated casting under the bridge. That's why he used to drift those jelly worms off the bridge.

Rich: [*laughing*] Yeah, I always wondered why he did that.

Billy: And then I started registering the bottom in my mind, you know, like putting together a map, your mind reads the bottom. You realize this is the drop, this is the ledge, the bump, the rock, working it out into the tide, because there were so many pieces of structure where you could find fish. And that's when you started fishing the bridge around that time, and when me and you started to fish, I think of everyone there, me and you beat them up the very most, you know, we had that bridge down pat in those days.

Rich: Like you said to me in the beginning, "If you want to cash in on the riches these bridges have to offer, then there's a price you're gonna have to pay." And the 3rd paid off in spades.

Billy: We had tremendous numbers on that bridge, and if you go through the whole year, there was no better month on that bridge than October, especially if you had a late moon, like right at the end of the month. Those fish would stage, and you would get that building bite, where every day the bite was more intense, with more fish than the day before. It would start three, four days before the moon and go four or five days after. If it was late enough in October, those fish would leave in one night. One night you kill'em, then poof, they're gone the next night, you know.

Rich: I've had them there until moons in mid-November, like a week before Thanksgiving. I'm guessing if the moon is too early in October, they just blow through it and keep eating.

Billy: No doubt about it. But it's always that building bite. That bridge had the most building bite I'd ever seen on any of the bridges. It was fierce, and then it was done.

Rich: Yeah… It was always such a bummer when I'd show up and there would be nothing but water. Then it was time to wait for the herring to show up front.

Billy: Do you remember those gigantic bluefish that would show up in October?

Rich: Yeah, I hated those things. I lost more bait-tails to them than I did to the bottom.

Billy: I had a twenty-four pound bluefish I weighed in off that bridge. I was with that kid Joey I told you about, who became a charter boat captain, well, that same night he had a twenty-one pound blue.

Rich: Wow… Twenty-four pounds, that's huge! The largest blue I ever caught was twenty-two pounds, thirteen ounces.

Billy: And that bridge had such a number of fish, I mean the giant bluefish showed up in October, the striped bass were always on the bridge in numbers, and when the weakfish showed up, I had numerous times where I caught all three in the same night. Big bluefish, big bass, not monster bass, twenty-five, thirty, thirty-two pound fish, you know, there were a lot of them on that bridge, and big weakfish in 98, in the twelve pound class when they were there. All in one night. And I did that a bunch of times. That bridge really drew fish to it like a magnet.

Rich: Believe it or not, I never caught a weakfish from up top on the third. I'd hear them feeding on the flats on the northwest side out to the point and catch them from shore, but never up top. I used to catch a ton off the flats on the southwest side of the second also. What was your biggest bass from the 3rd?

Billy: Forty-eight pounds. Got him down on the north side, sweeping sideways, you know, where you cast back under the bridge at an angle and let the bucktail sweep out sideways.

Rich: Yup, Wow! That's a good fish for the 3rd. I've never caught a forty from the 3rd. I mean I might have, because I don't keep fish usually. I've caught plenty of thirties, upper thirties, a couple of them might have even tipped forty maybe, who knows. I've caught some forties on the 2nd.

Billy: Another thing about the 3rd that was really impressive, it had way stronger tides than any other bridge.

Rich: Oh, way stronger!

Billy: So when you hooked a big fish, they really put up a good account of themselves, much more so than the other bridges. You catch that tide on a moon, when that tide is really cranking through there, a forty pound fish will feel absolutely huge, it would absolutely smoke you, especially when I was still fishing the Squidders, before I switched to the Newells. It would empty that reel before I could stop him!

Rich: Upper thirty pound fish used to run me off the bridge, deep into my spool sometimes.

Billy: That's what I'm saying! Upper thirties felt like fifty pound fish in the current… Listen to this, this is funny. I'm up there one night, it's like two days before the new moon, and the fish are committing suicide, I mean I was beating the crap out of these fish. And this guy Tommy is following me around, and he didn't know how to fish downtide, he snagged the bottom, was losing bucktails, didn't catch sh!t. At the end of the night I probably had forty-five or fifty fish, he didn't get a fish, not one! And he looks at me, and he was serious, I couldn't believe it, and he goes, "You know, if there were big fish here I would have caught one."

Rich: [*laughing*]

Billy: I was like, "Are you f&(kng kidding me, these fish were committing suicide and you couldn't catch one!" [*laughing*] If he was blind and I handed him the line he couldn't have caught one. [*more laughing*] I could be brutally honest at times. [*laughing*]

Rich: [*laughs*] Believe me, I know. I tell you what, it used to be a lot of fun when you and I were on that bridge at the same time. It was like a race to see who could catch the most fish. [*laughs*] We'd do forty, fifty fish each a night!

Billy: Yeah, I remember that, I'd be catching fish from one span and you'd leap frog over to the next span, and then as soon as I didn't hook up, I'd leap frog over you to the next span. We'd go back and forth, that was a lot of fun! And we knew which spans had more fish than the other spans, and then on the north side we would stand there free spooling back and pulling fish off the second ridge.

Rich: [*laughing*] The other guys on the bridge had no idea what the f we were even doing. We'd be standing there talking like we were having a cup of coffee, and all of sudden we'd set the hook on a fish. They couldn't figure out what was going on. I was dropping back one night and I had one guy who I was fairly friendly with, that guy I had told you about, come up to me after I had landed a fish and was walking back out. He said, "If you don't mind me asking, where did you catch that fish?" I pointed way out to the bump off the north side. He looked at me and said, "No really." I said, "I'm not sh!tting you, that's where I caught it, seriously!." He said, "Thanks for nothing!" and walked away pissed.

Billy: Hey, you weren't obligated to show anybody your tricks, you told him where you caught the fish, it was up to him to figure it out.

Rich: Yeah, But he was a good guy, I liked him. Didn't matter though because he didn't go far. He was going to find out, one way or the other, so I made it easy for him. Instead of loop casting under the bridge and hiding the free spooling drop back, I just lobbed my bait-tail right out in front of me, in plain sight, so that he could get a good look. Then I let my line run, making it obvious that I had not put my reel in gear, coming just short of holding my rod up and pointing to the spool. Then after bumping bottom, I made a show of putting the reel in gear and lifting my rod tip, then free spooling again, then in gear again, then getting hit on the lift and setting the hook, looking straight at him. After landing the fish, he came up and apologized for being nasty and thanked me for showing him how that was done. He was one of three people I ever showed anything to on the bridges. Funny thing is, I never once saw him use the drop back.

Billy: I bet I can tell you why. He probably couldn't find the pieces. Free spooling back isn't going to do anything unless you can land your bait on the pieces. He probably tried it a couple times, came up empty, and went back to what he knew.

Rich: Sounds about right.

Billy: I mean think about it, how many people took the time to learn every single detail, about every single span, what was under the bridge, in front of the bridge, away from the bridge, every square foot of bottom, how many people knew that bridge to that degree? You know there's only two, and that's you and me. And the worst part is the end comes, and all that knowledge, it's all in the garbage. I thought about that the other day. I spent fifty years learning these bridges, and it ain't worth a dime anymore. I mean the knowledge of knowing how to fish a bridge is worth it, you know what I mean, because a bridge, is a bridge, anywhere in the world. But our bridges were our bridges, and the 3rd Wantagh was the bridge that held the most fish for the most time, and was the hardest to learn.

Rich: For me, the 3rd Wantagh was very personal to me, because it was the bridge I caught my first bridge bass on, it was the most intimidating, in terms of me having to overcome some personal fears, and because I invested so much time and energy learning every inch of that bridge in order to maximize yield. [*laughs*] That's my business background speaking. But honestly, at the root of it, I'm a spot whore, even after I moved out from the bridges into the bay, I had to know where every freaking bass in the bay was, at all times. If I had fifty spots that all held fish, that wasn't enough, I wanted more. And that's the way I was with the 3rd. From as far back under the bridge as I could cast, to as far as I could drop back downtide, the area of a football field, I needed to know every nook and cranny that a bass might hold in. And that's why I felt such an intimate attachment to that bridge… I owned that bridge, I had made it mine, and when they tore it down, it really hurt. It was like you said, all the excitement of discovery, the compiling of knowledge, flushed right down the crapper. There will never be another bridge like the 3rd Wantagh Bridge.

Billy: You got that right.

218

They ripped the roadway off and took it away in pieces on barges, then the pilings went, and then nothing for a while. I went down and fished some of the structure I knew so well from shore, but the limited number of fish I was able to catch within the reach of my casts, didn't help my sense of loss. I poked around under the temporary bridge and found a few spots that produced some fish, but again, it was too little to fill the void. It took them thirteen years to finish the replacement bridge and it wasn't built over the bottom where the original 3rd was. It was built about sixty feet to the east and from what I learned, all the original bottom had been destroyed in the process of the rebuilding, which had not gone well.

The original company defaulted on its contract when it was unable to sink the pilings to the specified depth and ran into money problems. The second company eventually finished the bridge, but apparently there are still issues with the pilings. The original plan called for a catwalk to be built beneath the bridge, running shore to shore, for us fishermen to fish from. They probably figured it was better to have us underneath and out of the way, then up top and a constant distraction. So at least we had that to look forward to. But in true New York fashion, they ultimately changed the plan to the much vaunted "Green Island Fishing Pier", which turned out to be a zig zag pier that runs along the north shore line, and is useless for anything except catching baby Seabass and Porgies.

Billy continued his quest for a world record striped bass, endlessly patrolling the shadow lines of the up front bridges and racking up impressive numbers of big fish.

He even managed to duplicate his feat of four fifties and a sixty in one night again. I became a fixture at the 2nd Wantagh for a while, from the top, but also from my rock on the southeast shore, fishing the ridge at the second span. I actually came to really enjoy the challenge of catching fish from down there, despite nearly bashing my brains in when my line broke that one night. It was real throw down, brawl type fishing, and it helped me work off my frustration at losing the 3rd. The only drawback was I didn't like getting smoked by some of the big fish I hooked. I would have used stand up tuna gear if I could have casted it far enough.

I also fished some of the up front bridges, mostly the Meadowbrook, the Fundy from down below, in a location known as the sand pit, and the Loop Parkway Bridge, particularly late in the year when the herring showed up. We used to catch some really big fish live lining blueback herring. To catch the herring I would make a herring tree rig, which was basically the same idea as a mackerel tree. I would use a six-foot conventional rig spooled with twenty-pound mono. I would tie four dropper loops in the line and then an overhand knot at the bottom for the sinker. To the dropper loops, I attached standard flounder hooks and wrapped the shafts tightly with tin foil. To the overhand knot at the bottom, I would usually attach a two or three-ounce sinker. Jigging this six-feet or so under the lights was usually sufficient for multiple hookups. The extra herring went into the pockets of my six-pocket camo pants, which became so stiff with fish slime and scales, that I could stand them up in the corner at night when I took them off.

The Big Dog was rigged with a three-way swivel, simply because I didn't trust a dropper loop to hold a big fish. The bottom swivel had three-feet of twenty-pound mono terminated in an overhand knot for a six-ounce sinker. The side swivel had a 8/0 Mustad live bait hook connected via a one-foot length of fifty-pound mono leader material, and the top swivel was tied direct to the fifty-pound Ande mono running line. All connections were made using a palomar knot.

As soon as I caught a live herring, I would reel it up, stow any extras in my pockets, put the herring on the hook of my Big Dog, and drop it straight to the bottom. I usually didn't have to wait long, as bass would suck these in like candy. I would feel the herring start panicking at the end of the line, then the thump of the bass, and after setting the hook, it was game on. Most of the time the fish would run off the bridge, because this was outgoing fishing, with the current moving away from you. But sometimes, some of the bigger fish ran uptide under the bridge and required some coaxing to get them turned around and out away from the bridge.

After you got your fish under control, it came time to land it, and the Loop Parkway Bridge was one of the worst bridges when it came to landing fish. While you walked your fish down, you let it stay off the bridge quite a ways. Then you put your reel in free spool, but controlling the tension and amount of line you let out with your thumb, you had to run all the way to the end of the bridge and around the railing. From there, you put your reel in gear, ran down hill on a path, while reeling in slack and keeping tension on the line, which took you to a large minefield of broken concrete slabs and rebar rods sticking out everywhere. Here your line would no doubt be interwoven in some of the rebar, so you had to carefully pick your way over the concrete, untangling your line as you go, until you reached the shore. At that point, you landed your fish as best you could, as there were no convenient landing rocks. It was not a user-friendly place to land big fish.

This fishing usually took place around the end of November and into December, and depended on the herring showing up. Some years it took patience, as the herring didn't show up like clockwork, but when they did, they usually drew some late season big fish with them, so it was well worth the effort. It was also cold fishing, the kind of cold that could test your endurance. Nothing was worse than getting a cold snap when the fishing was hot. You knew the fish were only going to be there for a very short time, so you did whatever you had to do, to deal with the cold. I would catch one fish and then go into my car and scream for five minutes, as I thawed my hands out in front of the heat vents. And then I'd go out and catch another.

But ultimately my attention began to wander away from the west end bridges some. I began to fish a couple of the bridges out east, and I also became fascinated with the bay system, first around the west end bridges, but eventually the entire south shore. My inner spot whore took over and I became obsessed with what I was finding in the bays. This was right at the apex of the striped bass recovery, and it was almost as if there wasn't enough water to fit all the striped bass in existence at that time.

222

My spot manual has one hundred and eighty-seven pages in it, plus many pages of scribbled notes and pictures that never got cataloged, but that's another story for another book. I also spent more time on the beach. For quite a number of years I was bouncing around like a rubber ball and I kept myself well plugged in.

When the new 3rd Wantagh was finally completed, I made it a point to go out there with the Big Dog and give it an initiation. For me it was a moral imperative, a promise I had made to myself years before. On a cold, fall week night, I drove my Blazer into the Green Island parking area, which is on the northwest side. I wasn't even sure it was open yet. I jumped a few railings, and walked out onto the northwest side of the bridge. I walked all the way over the bridge to the approximate area where I had caught my first bass from the original bridge. There were a couple of dim lights on the bridge, which did little to improve my mood. To make the initiation official, I undid my pants, whipped out my dick, and anointed the bridge by pissing on the fresh pavement. As I stowed my junk, I watched in silence as steam rose from the wet areas and drifted off in the night breeze.

The railing they had used for this bridge had four rails and was chest high, the same railing they had put up on all the other bridges, so I had to stand on the bottom rail, just to reach over the top rail to cast. It was very uncomfortable and clumsy, and I immediately became annoyed. I made two loop casts, trying to find the bottom, and was unable to do so on either cast. Between trying to balance myself on the bottom rail while casting and fishing, having no idea where the pilings were, and no clue as to the water depth, the whole exercise seemed completely pointless and irritating. All it was doing was making me remember what I had lost. But it was an imperative, a promise I had made, that I properly initiate the new bridge, and I had needed to complete the cycle. So with that task now out of the way, I walked back to my truck, and never set foot on that bridge again.

Epilogue…

Somewhere around 2010, I was probably one of the first people to predict the future decline in the striped bass stocks that we are witnessing today, in 2025. I had started looking at YOY data from the Chesapeake and Hudson stocks and was also looking at the data that the ASMFC had, and how they were managing the resource. I started trending that data out, and I didn't like what I saw for the future. I started talking about this on Noreast.com, whom I was a moderator for at the time, and members literally jumped down my online throat. Now, fishing was still really good at that time, so it was kind of understandable, because people were only basing their opinions on their personal experiences. I'm catching fish, nope, nothing wrong here.

But numbers don't lie, and over time the cracks began to emerge. The fish became less evenly spread, traditional bites began to be less dependable, or disappear altogether, and eventually it came down to some fishermen had fish, and everybody else had nothing, or had to hope that those fish would show up for them. The

Chesapeake had relatively successful year classes in 2011 and again in 2015, and the Hudson chipped in a little, but in the last five years, neither the Chesapeake, or the Hudson, has had a successful year class. Not one.

The striped bass that fishermen are catching today are coming primarily from the 2011 and the 2015 year classes. When those are gone, there's not much behind to take their place. And the ASMFC doesn't even want to talk about mycobacteriosis, the bass killer that every fisherman should read up on and know about. Instead, the ASMFC would rather lay myco's forty-seven percent mortality rate at the feet of recreational release mortality, which is absolute BS!

What is my point? Well, first off I don't see the striped bass ever recovering to the levels that we had post moratorium, through the 90s, and into the first decade plus of 2K. That kind of lightning only strikes once. Then there's the nine west end bridges, many rebuilt with the chest high railings, bottoms dredged clean, and no fish on them anyway. It's a type of fishing that has seen its day come and go, never to return.

So my point is that throughout all of our conversations, one thing kept distilling and coming to the surface. And that was that Billy and I considered ourselves incredibly fortunate we were able to experience the unbelievable fishing that the nine west end bridges provided us. Fueled by the remarkable striped bass recovery that took place, it was the kind of fishing that dreams are made of, and we got to do it. Nobody will ever again experience the numbers of striped bass we caught nightly, and nobody will ever come close to matching the number of striped bass over fifty pounds that Billy has caught. But unfortunately he never got his world record bass. Today, we're in our early seventies and of course, we still fish. As for me, since moving to the Virginia Beach area twelve years ago, the decline in the striped bass stocks has been supplanted by catching the big Red Drum that inhabit these waters. Billy, on the other hand, has his mind set on catching a world record Bluegill 😊

One Last Funny Bit

It's March 8th 2025, the day before we set our clocks ahead, not that that has anything to do with the story, and Billy calls me. He tells me that earlier in the day he went down to the Lindenhurst Fishing Show for a bit. For those who don't know, the Lindenhurst Fishing Show is one of the smaller fishing shows / flea markets on Long Island, that help pass the time during the colder months until the Striped Bass and other fishing seasons start. So, Billy is looking at some stuff at one of the tables, and somebody comes up from behind and taps him on the shoulder. He turns around and there's a man, somewhere in his late fifties or so, who Billy has never seen before in his life. and he's looking Billy straight in the eyes. After a few awkward seconds, the man finally asks Billy if he ever knew anybody who mated on the Commodore.

Now that got Billy's attention immediately. Billy tells him that he knew all the mates, because he had worked as a mate on the Commodore in his younger years, and that it was actually his first job. The guy gets all excited.

"I knew it was you!" the guy exclaims. "I recognized you right away, my Dad and I used to fish on the Commodore when I was just a kid, you haven't changed a bit!"

"Haven't changed a bit?" Billy says, "I'm seventy years old, what have you been drinking?" and starts laughing. Billy said he turned out to be a nice guy and they talked about the days back on the Commodore for a while. I said to Billy that he must have recognized you from the mustache you've had since you were 6 years old. Billy told me that it was actually 17 years old, and that he has never shaved it off once.

Acknowledgements

A special thanks to Billy "the Greek" Legakis, for his input into this book, but it goes way beyond that. Simply put, no Billy, no book, no bridge fishing for me, probably a whole different paradigm on fishing in general, as well as the impact he's had on my personal life. I consider myself most fortunate to count him as a friend. I'd would also like to thank John Mlodynia for the excellent, in-depth job of proof reading and editing he did on this book. As a skilled fisherman with editing skills, nothing escaped his critical eye. Thanks also go to my wife for her tolerance while I was MIA during this whole process, and finally, thank you to all those who have been pushing me for years to write a book. Rear cover photo by Billy Legakis. Author photo w/ red drum curtesy of Andrew Kumjian. Front cover photo adapted from WIKIMEDIA COMMONS File: "Loop Parkway - Long Creek Bridge from the water 03 (9341531282).jpg" by Joe Mabel and is licensed under CC BY-SA 3.0 Unported https://creativecommons.org/licenses/by-sa/3.0/deed.en

About The Author

Rich Troxler, also known as "richtrox" is a surf fisherman and the host of the YouTube channel *The View From The Beach*, where he shares his extensive knowledge of surf fishing gained from nearly 50 years of fishing the northeastern shores and bays of the US coast. He was the long time moderator of the Surf Fishing Board on Nor'east Saltwater Magazine, where he provided content in addition to his moderating duties. He also had his own board on Stripers 247, where he was the only person who could post content, and has provided close to a book's worth of content there alone. He has also written numerous articles and short stories that have been published in the popular online magazine Surfcaster's Journal. He has done several seminars and been the guest speaker at fishing clubs, and has appeared on podcasts, such as Surfcast Podcast with Jerry Audet of In Deep Outdoors. Rich was also one of the earliest fishermen to warn of the current decline in the bass stocks, all based on his analysis and trending of the data at that time. He produced a video that is over an hour long of his findings that is on his YouTube Channel. As a fisherman, Rich has always been known for his secretive and solitary approach to the sport, practicing C&R, and only keeping damaged fish for the table. In addition to the decades of knowledge fishing the west end bridges of Long Island, he possesses an intimate knowledge of Long Island's South Shore Bay system, and was known for always being able to find fish. Besides fishing, Rich is a muti-instrumentalist and composer, who has recorded and produced several albums. You can visit his website at: www.richtroxler.net to see what's streamed, where to buy, and for a whole lot more info on him. He now resides with his wife in Chesapeake, VA. where he enjoys catching fifty pound Red Drum from the Virginia Beach shore, as well as Puppy Drum and Speckled Trout from his kayak on beautiful Lynnhaven Bay.